Letters of Marque

Letters of Marque

The Works of

Rudyard Kipling

Published by

GYAN

Gyan Publishing House
5, Ansari Road
Daryaganj, New Delhi-110002
Phone: 011-47034999, 9811692060
E-mail: books@gyanbooks.com

Distribution Network

gyanbooks.com

India, USA, Canada, UK, Australia, France

ISBN: 978-81-212-8226-0 (PB)
First Published, 1899

2nd Impression 2023

Printed at: Gyan Press, Delhi.

LETTERS OF MARQUE
Author: RUDYARD KIPLING

Rudyard Kipling

Photogravure — From photograph

Letters of Marque

By Rudyard Kipling

Author of
"Soldiers Three," "The Day's Work,"
"Under the Deodars," etc.

Illustrated

New York and Boston
H. M. Caldwell Company
Publishers

LIST OF ILLUSTRATIONS

LETTERS OF MARQUE

I.

Of the beginning of Things—Of the Taj and the Globe-Trotter—The Young Man from Manchester and certain Moral Reflections.

EXCEPT for those who, under compulsion of a sick certificate, are flying Bombaywards, it is good for every man to see some little of the great Indian Empire and the strange folk who move about it. It is good to escape for a time from the House of Rimmon—be it office or cutchery—and to go abroad under no more exacting master than personal inclination, and with no more definite plan of travel than has the horse, escaped from pasture, free upon the country side. The first result of such freedom is extreme bewilderment, and the second reduces the freed to a state of mind which, for his sins, must be the normal portion of the Globe-Trotter—the man who "does" kingdoms in days and writes books upon them in weeks. And this desperate facility is not as strange as it seems. By the time that an Englishman has come by sea and rail *via* America, Japan, Singapore, and Ceylon to India, he can—these eyes have seen him do so —master in five minutes the intricacies of the *Indian Bradshaw*, and tell an old resident exactly how and where the trains run. Can we wonder that the intoxication of success in hasty assimilation should make him overbold, and that he should try to grasp—but a full account of the insolent Globe-Trotter must be reserved. He is worthy of a book. Given absolute freedom for a month the mind, as I have said, fails to take in the situation and, after much debate, contents itself with following in old and well-beaten ways —paths that we in India have no time to tread, but must leave to the country-cousin who wears his *pagri* tail-fashion down his back, and says "cabman" to the driver of the ticca-ghari.

Now Jeypore from the Anglo-Indian point of view is a station on the Rajputana-Malwa line, on the way to Bombay, where half an hour is allowed for dinner, and where there ought to be more protection from the sun than at present exists. Some few, more learned than the rest, know that garnets come from Jeypore, and here the limits of our wisdom are set. We do not, to quote the Calcutta shopkeeper, come out "for the good of our 'ealth," and what touring we accomplish is for the most part off the line of rail.

For these reasons, and because he wished to study our winter birds of passage, one of the few thousand Englishmen in India, on a date and in a place which have no concern with the story, sacrificed all his self-respect and became—at enormous personal inconvenience—a Globe-Trotter going to Jeypore, and leaving behind him for a little while all that old and well-known life in which Commissioners and Deputy Commissioners, Governors and Lieutenant-Governors, Aides-de-Camp, Colonels and their wives, Majors, Captains and Subalterns after their kind move and rule and govern and squabble and fight and sell each other's horses, and tell wicked stories of their neighbours. But before he had fully settled into his part or accustomed himself to saying "Please take out this luggage" to the coolies at the stations, he saw from the train the Taj wrapped in the mists of the morning.

There is a story of a Frenchman "who feared not God, nor regarded man," sailing to Egypt for the express purpose of scoffing at the Pyramids and—though this is hard to believe—at the great Napoleon who had warred under their shadow! It is on record that that blasphemous Gaul came to the Great Pyramid and wept through mingled reverence and contrition, for he sprang from an emotional race. To understand his feelings, it is necessary to have read a great deal too much about the Taj, its design and proportions, to have seen execrable pictures of it at the Simla Fine Arts Exhibition, to have had its praises sung by superior and travelled friends till the brain loathed the repetition of the word, and then, sulky with want of sleep, heavy-eyed, unwashen and chilled, to come upon it suddenly. Under these circumstances everything you will concede, is in favour of a cold, critical and not too impartial verdict. As the Englishman leaned out of the carriage he saw first an opal-tinted cloud on the horizon, and later certain towers. The mists lay on the ground, so that the splendour seemed to be floating free of the earth; and the mists rose in the background, so that at no time could everything be seen clearly. Then as the train sped forward, and the mists shifted and the sun shone upon the mists, the Taj took a hundred new shapes, each perfect and each beyond description. It was the Ivory Gate through which all good dreams come; it was the realization of the "glimmering halls of dawn" that Tennyson sings of; it was veritably the "aspiration fixed," the "sigh made stone" of a lesser poet; and over

The Taj Mahal.

and above concrete comparisons, it seemed the embodiment of all things pure, all things holy and all things unhappy. That was the mystery of the building. It may be that the mists wrought the witchery, and that the Taj seen in the dry sunlight is only as guide books say a noble structure. The Englishman could not tell, and has made a vow that he will never go nearer the spot for fear of breaking the charm of the unearthly pavilions.

It may be, too, that each must view the Taj for himself with his own eyes; working out his own interpretation of the sight. It is certain that no man can in cold blood and colder ink set down his impressions if he has been in the least moved.

To the one who watched and wondered that November morning the thing seemed full of sorrow—the sorrow of the man who built it for the woman he loved, and the sorrow of the workmen who died in the building—used up like cattle. And in the face of this sorrow the Taj flushed in the sunlight and was beautiful, after the beauty of a woman who has done no wrong.

Here the train ran in under the walls of Agra Fort, and another train—of thought incoherent as that written above—came to an end. Let those who scoff at overmuch enthusiasm look at the

Taj and thenceforward be dumb. It is well on the threshold of a journey to be taught reverence and awe.

But there is no reverence in the Globe-Trotter: he is brazen. A Young Man from Manchester was travelling to Bombay in order—how the words hurt!—to be home by Christmas. He had come through America, New Zealand, and Australia, and finding that he had ten days to spare at Bombay, conceived the modest idea of "doing India." "I don't say that I've done it all; but you may say that I've seen a good deal." Then he explained that he had been "much pleased" at Agra, "much pleased" at Delhi and, last profanation, "very much pleased" at the Taj. Indeed he seemed to be going through life just then "much pleased" at everything. With rare and sparkling originality he remarked that India was a "big place," and that there were many things to buy. Verily, this Young Man must have been a delight to the Delhi boxwallahs. He had purchased shawls and embroidery "to the tune of" a certain number of rupees duly set forth, and he had purchased jewellery to another tune. These were gifts for friends at home, and he considered them "very Eastern." If silver filigree work modelled on Palais Royal patterns, or aniline blue scarves be "Eastern," he had succeeded in his heart's desire. For some inscrutable end it has been decreed that man shall take a delight in making his fellow-man miserable. The Englishman began to point out gravely the probable extent to which the Young Man from Manchester had been swindled, and the Young Man said:—"By Jove! You don't say so. I hate being done! If there's anything I hate it's being done!"

He had been so happy in the "thought of getting home by Christmas," and so charmingly communicative as to the members of his family for whom such and such gifts were intended, that the Englishman cut short the record of fraud and soothed him by saying that he had not been so very badly "done" after all. This consideration was misplaced, for, his peace of mind restored, the Young Man from Manchester looked out of the window and, waving his hand over the Empire generally, said:—"I say! Look here! All those wells are wrong you know." The wells were on the wheel and inclined plane system; but he objected to the incline, and said that it would be much better for the bullocks if they walked on level ground. Then light dawned upon him, and he said:—"I suppose it's to exercise all their muscles. Y'know a canal horse is no use after he has been on the tow path for some time. He can't walk anywhere but on the flat y'know, and I suppose it's just the same with bullocks." The spurs of the Aravalis, under which the train was running, had evidently suggested this brilliant idea which passed uncontradicted, for the Englishman was looking out of the window.

If one were bold enough to generalise after the manner of Globe-Trotters, it would be easy to build up a theory on the well incident to account for the apparent insanity of some of our cold weather visitors. Even the Young Man from Manchester could evolve a complete idea for the training of well-bullocks in the East at thirty-seconds' notice. How much the more could a cultivated observer from, let us say, an English constituency blunder and pervert and mangle! We in this country have no time to work out the notion, which is worthy of the consideration of some leisurely Teuton intellect.

Envy may have prompted a too bitter judgment of the Young Man from Manchester; for, as the train bore him from Jeypore to Ahmedabad, happy in "his getting home by Christmas," pleased as a child with his Delhi atrocities, pink-cheeked, whiskered and superbly self-confident, the Englishman, whose home for the time was a dâk bungaloathesome hotel, watched his departure regretfully; for he knew exactly to what sort of genial, cheery British household, rich in untravelled kin, that Young Man was speeding. It is pleasant to play at globe-trotting; but to enter fully into the spirit of the piece, one must also be going home for Christmas.

II.

Shows the Charm of Rajputana and of Jeypore, the City of the Globe-Trotter—Of its Founder and its Embellishment—Explains the use and destiny of the Stud-Bred, and fails to explain many more important matters.

IF any part of a land strewn with dead men's bones have a special claim to distinction, Rajputana, as the cockpit of India, stands first. East of Suez men do not build towers on the tops of hills for the sake of the view, nor do they stripe the mountain sides with bastioned stone walls to keep in cattle. Since the beginning of time, if we are to credit the legends, there was fighting—heroic fighting—at the foot of the Aravalis, and beyond in the great deserts of sand penned by those kindly mountains from spreading over the heart of India. The "Thirty-six Royal Races" fought as royal races know how to do, Chohan with Rahtor, brother against brother, son against father. Later—but excerpts from the tangled tale of force, fraud, cunning, desperate love and more desperate revenge, crime worthy of demons and virtues fit for gods, may be found, by all who care to look, in the book of the man who loved the Rajputs and gave a life's labours in their behalf. From Delhi to Abu, and from the Indus to the Chambul, each yard of ground has witnessed slaughter, pillage and rapine. But, to-day, the capital of the State, that Dhola Rae, son of Soora Singh, hacked out more than nine hundred years ago with the sword from some weaker ruler's realm, is lighted with gas, and possesses many striking and English peculiarities which will be shown in their proper place.

Dhola Rae was killed in due time, and for nine hundred years Jeypore, torn by the intrigues of unruly princes and princelings, fought Asiatically.

When and how Jeypore became a feudatory of British power, and in what manner we put a slur upon Rajput honour—punctilious as the honour of the Pathan—are matters of which the Globe-Trotter knows more than we do. He "reads up"—to quote his own words—a city before he comes to us, and, straightway going to another city, forgets, or, worse still, mixes what he has learnt—so that in the end he writes down the Rajput a Mahratta, says that Lahore is in the North-West Provinces and was once the capital of Sivaji, and piteously demands a "guide-book on all India, a thing that you can carry in your trunk y'know—that gives you plain descriptions of things without mixing you up." Here is a chance for a writer of discrimination and void of conscience!

But to return to Jeypore—a pink city set on the border of a blue lake, and surrounded by the low red spurs of the Aravalis—a city to see and to puzzle over. There was once a ruler of the State, called Jey Singh, who lived in the days of Aurungzeb, and did him service with foot and horse. He must have been the Solomon of Rajputana, for through the forty-four years of his reign his "wisdom remained with him." He led armies, and when fighting was over, turned to literature; he intrigued desperately and successfully, but found time to gain a deep insight into astronomy, and, by what remains above ground now, we can tell that "whatsoever his eyes desired, he kept not from him." Knowing his own worth, he deserted the city of Amber founded by Dhola Rae among the hills, and, six miles further, in the open plain, bade one Vedyadhar, his architect, build a new city, as seldom Indian city was built before—with huge streets straight as an arrow, sixty yards broad, and cross-streets broad and straight. Many years afterwards the good people of America builded their towns after this pattern, but knowing nothing of Jey Singh, they took all the credit to themselves.

He built himself everything that pleased him, palaces and gardens and temples, and then died, and was buried under a white marble tomb on a hill overlooking the city. He was a traitor, if history speak truth, to his own kin, and he was an accomplished murderer, but he did his best to check infanticide; he reformed the Mahomedan calendar; he piled up a superb library and he made Jeypore a marvel.

Later on came a successor, educated and enlightened by all the lamps of British Progress, and converted the city of Jey Singh into a surprise—a big, bewildering, practical joke. He laid down sumptuous *trottoirs* of hewn stone, and central carriage drives, also of hewn stone, in the main street; he, that is to say, Colonel Jacob, the Superintending Engineer of the State, devised a water-supply for the city and studded the ways with stand-pipes. He built gas-works, set a-foot a School of Art, a Museum, all the things in fact which are necessary to Western municipal welfare and comfort, and saw that they were the best of their kind. How much Colonel Jacob has done, not only for the good of Jeypore city but for the good of the State at large, will never be known, because the officer in question is one of the not small class who resolutely refuse to talk about their own work. The result of the good work is that the old and the new, the rampantly raw and the sullenly old, stand cheek-by-jowl in startling contrast. Thus, the branded bull trips over the rails of a steel tramway which brings out the city rubbish; the lacquered and painted *ruth,* behind the two little stag-like trotting bullocks, catches its primitive wheels in the cast-iron gas-lamp post with the brass nozzle a-top, and all Rajputana, gaily-clad, small-turbaned, swaggering Rajputana, circulates along the magnificent pavements.

The fortress-crowned hills look down upon the strange medley. One of them bears on its flank in huge white letters the cheery inscript "Welcome!" This was made when the Prince of Wales visited Jeypore to shoot his first tiger; but the average traveller of to-day may appropriate the message to himself, for Jeypore takes great care of strangers and shows them all courtesy. This, by the way, demoralises the Globe-Trotter, whose first cry is:—"Where can we get horses? Where can we get elephants? Who is the man to write to for all these things?"

Thanks to the courtesy of the Maharaja, it is possible to see everything, but for the incurious who object to being driven through their sights,

Street Scene in Jeypore.

a journey down any one of the great main streets is a day's delightful occupation. The view is as unobstructed as that of the Champs Elysees; but in place of the white-stone fronts of Paris, rises a long line of open-work screen-wall, the prevailing tone of which is pink—caramel pink, but house-owners have unlimited license to decorate their tenements as they please. Jeypore, broadly considered, is Hindu, and her architecture of the riotous many-arched type which even the Globe-Trotter after a short time learns to call Hindu. It is neither temperate nor noble, but it satisfies the general desire for something that "really looks Indian." A perverse taste for low company drew the Englishman from the pavement—to walk upon a real stone pavement is in itself a privilege—up a side-street where he assisted at a quail fight and found the low-caste Rajput a cheery and affable soul. The owner of the losing quail was a sowar in the Maharaja's army. He explained that his pay was six rupees a month paid bi-monthly. He was cut the cost of his khaki blouse, brown-leather accoutrements and jack-boots; lance, saddle, sword, and horse were given free. He refused to say for how many months in the year he was drilled, and said vaguely that his duties were mainly escort ones, and he had no fault to find with them. The defeat of his quail had vexed him, and he desired the Sahib to understand that the sowars of His Highness's army could ride. A clumsy attempt at a compliment so fired his martial blood that he climbed into his saddle, and then and there insisted on showing off his horsemanship. The road was narrow, the lance was long, and the horse was a big one, but no one objected, and the Englishman sat him down on a doorstep and watched the fun. The horse seemed in some shadowy way familiar. His head was not the lean head of the Kathiawar, nor his crest the crest of the Marwarri, and his fore-legs did not seem to belong to the stony district. "Where did he come from?" The sowar pointed northward and said "from Amritsar," but he pronounced it "Armtzar." Many horses had been brought at the spring fairs in the Punpab; they cost about Rs. 200 each, perhaps more, the sowar could not say. Some came from Hissar and some from other places beyond Delhi. They were very good horses. "That horse there," he pointed to one a little distance down the street, "is the son of a big Sirkar horse—the kind that the Sirkar make for breeding horses—so high!" The owner of "that horse" swaggered up, jaw-bandaged and cat-moustached, and bade the Englishman look at his mouth; bought, of course, when a *butcha.* Both men together said that the Sahib had better examine the Maharaja Sahib's stable, where there were hundreds of horses—huge as elephants or tiny as sheep.

To the stables the Englishman accordingly went, knowing beforehand what he would find, and wondering whether the Sirkar's "big horses" were meant to get mounts for Rajput sowars. The Maharaja's stables are royal in size and appointments. The enclosure round which they stand must be about half a mile long—it allows ample space for exercising, besides paddocks for the colts. The horses, about two hundred and fifty, are bedded in pure white sand—bad for the coat if they roll, but good for the feet—the pickets are of white marble, the heel-ropes in every case of good sound rope, and in every case the stables are exquisitely clean. Each stall contains above the manger, a curious little bunk for the syce who, if he uses the accommodation, must assuredly die once each hot weather.

A journey round the stables is saddening, for the attendants are very anxious to strip their charges, and the stripping shows so much. A few men in India are credited with the faculty of never forgetting a horse they have once seen, and of knowing the produce of every stallion they have met. The Englishman would have given something for their company at that hour. His knowledge of horseflesh was very limited; but he felt certain that more than one or two of the sleek, perfectly groomed country-breds should have been justifying their existence in the ranks of the British cavalry, instead of eating their heads off on six seers of gram and one of *goor* per diem. But they had all been honestly bought and honestly paid for; and there was nothing in the wide world to prevent His Highness, if he wished to do so, from sweeping up the pick and pride of all the horses in the Punjab. The attendants appeared to take a wicked delight in saying "eshtud-bred" very loudly and with unnecessary emphasis as they threw back the loin-cloth. Sometimes they were wrong, but in too many cases they were right.

The Englishman left the stables and the great central maidan where a nervous Biluchi was being taught, by a perfect network of ropes, to "monkey jump," and went out into the streets reflecting on the working of horse-breeding operations under the Government of India, and the advantages of having unlimited money wherewith to profit by other people's mistakes.

Then, as happened to the great Tartarin of

Tarescon in Milianah, wild beasts began to roar, and a crowd of little boys laughed. The lions of Jeypore are tigers, caged in a public place for the sport of the people, who hiss at them and disturb their royal feelings. Two or three of the six great brutes are magnificent. All of them are short-tempered, and the bars of their captivity not too strong. A pariah-dog was furtively trying to scratch out a fragment of meat from between the bars of one of the cages, and the occupant tolerated him. Growing bolder—the starveling growled; the tiger struck at him with his paw and the dog fled howling with fear. When he returned, he brought two friends with him, and the trio mocked the captive from a distance.

It was not a pleasant sight and suggested Globe-Trotters—gentlemen who imagine that "more curricles" should come at their bidding, and on being undeceived become abusive.

III.

Does not in any sort describe the Dead City of Amber, but gives detailed information of a Cotton Press.

AND what shall be said of Amber, Queen of the Pass—the city that Jey Singh bade his people slough as snakes cast their skins? The Globe-Trotter will assure you that it must be "done" before anything else, and the Globe-Trotter is, for once, perfectly correct. Amber lies between six and seven miles from Jeypore among the "tumbled fragments of the hills," and is reachable by so prosaic a conveyance as a ticca-ghari, and so uncomfortable a one as an elephant. *He* is provided by the Maharaja, and the people who make India their prey are apt to accept his services as a matter of course.

Rise very early in the morning, before the stars have gone out, and drive through the sleeping city till the pavement gives place to cactus and sand, and educational and enlightened institutions to mile upon mile of semi-decayed Hindu temples—brown and weather-beaten—running down to the shores of the great Man Sagar Lake, wherein are more ruined temples, palaces and fragments of causeways. The water-birds have their home in the half-submerged arcades and the *mugger* nuzzles the shafts of the pillars. It is a fitting prelude to the desolation of Amber. Beyond the Man Sagar the road of to-day climbs up-hill, and by its side runs the huge stone-causeway of yesterday—blocks sunk in concrete. Down this path the swords of Amber went out to kill. A triple wall rings the city, and, at the third gate, the road drops into the valley of Amber. In the half light of dawn, a great city sunk between hills and built round three sides of a lake is dimly visible, and one waits to catch the hum that should rise from it as the day breaks. The air in the valley is bitterly chill. With the growing light, Amber stands revealed, and the traveller sees that it is a city that will never wake. A few *meenas* live in huts at the end of the valley, but the temples, the shrines, the palaces, and the tiers-on-tiers of houses are desolate. Trees grow in and split open the walls, the windows are filled with brushwood, and the cactus chokes the street. The Englishman made his way up the side of the hill to the great palace that overlooks everything except the red fort of Jeighur, guardian of Amber. As the elephant swung up the steep roads paved with stone and built out on the sides of the hill, the Englishman looked into empty houses where the little grey squirrel sat and scratched its ears. The peacock walked upon the house-tops and the blue pigeon roosted within. He passed under iron-studded gates whereof the hinges were eaten out with rust, and by walls plumed and crowned with grass, and under more gateways, till, at last, he reached the palace and came suddenly into a great quadrangle where two blinded, arrogant stallions, covered with red and gold trappings, screamed and neighed at each other from opposite ends of the vast space. For a little time these were the only visible living beings, and they were in perfect accord with the spirit of the spot. Afterwards certain workmen appeared, for it seems that the Maharaja keeps the old palace of his forefathers in good repair, but they were modern and mercenary, and with great difficulty were detached from the skirts of the traveller. A somewhat extensive experience of palace-seeing had taught him that it is best to see palaces alone, for the Oriental as a guide is undiscriminating and sets too great a store on corrugated iron-roofs and glazed drain-pipes.

So the Englishman went into this palace built of stone, bedded on stone, springing out of scarped rock, and reached by stone ways—nothing but stone. Presently, he stumbled across a little temple of Kali, a gem of marble tracery and inlay, very dark and, at that hour of the morning, very cold.

If, as Violet-le-Duc tells us to believe, a building reflects the character of its inhabitants, it must be impossible for one reared in an Eastern palace to think straightly or speak freely or—but here the annals of Rajputana contradict the theory—to act openly. The crampt and darkened rooms, the narrow smooth-walled passages with recesses where a man might wait for his enemy unseen, the maze of ascending and descending stairs leading nowhither, the ever present screens of marble tracery that may hide or reveal so much,—all these things breathe of plot and counter-plot, league and intrigue. In a living palace where the sightseer knows and feels that there are human beings everywhere, and that he is followed by scores of unseen eyes, the impression is almost unendurable. In a dead palace—a cemetery of loves and hatreds done with hundreds of years ago, and of plottings that had for their end—though the grey beards who plotted knew it not—the coming of the British tourist with guide-book and sunhat—oppression gives place to simply impertinent curiosity. The Englishman wandered into all parts of the palace, for there was no one to stop him—not even the ghosts of the dead Ranis—through ivory-studded doors, into the women's quarters, where a stream of water once flowed over a chiselled marble channel. A creeper had set its hands upon the lattice here, and there was dust of old nests in one of the niches in the wall. Did the lady of light virtue who managed to become possessed of so great a portion of Jey Singh's library ever set her dainty feet in the trim garden of the Hall of Pleasure beyond the screen-work? Was it in the forty-pillared Hall of Audience that the order went forth that the Chief of Birjooghar was to be slain, and from what wall did the King look out when the horsemen clattered up the steep stone path to the palace, bearing on their saddle-bows the heads of the bravest of Rajore? There were questions innumerable to be asked in each court and keep and cell; aye, but the only answer was the cooing of the pigeons on the walls.

If a man desired beauty, there was enough and to spare in the palace; and of strength more than enough. By inlay and carved marble, by glass and colour, the Kings who took their pleasure in that now desolate pile, made all that their eyes rested upon royal and superb. But any description of the artistic side of the palace, if it were not impossible, would be wearisome. The wise man will visit it when time and occasion serve, and will then, in some small measure, understand what must have been the riotous, sumptuous, murderous life to which our Governors and Lieutenant-Governors, Commissioners and Deputy Commissioners, Colonels and Captains and the Subalterns after their kind, have put an end.

From the top of the palace you may read if you please the Book of Ezekiel written in stone upon the hillside. Coming up, the Englishman had seen the city from below or on a level. He now looked into its very heart—the heart that had ceased to beat. There was no sound of men or cattle, or grind-stones in those pitiful streets—nothing but the cooing of the pigeons. At first it seemed that the palace was not ruined at all—that presently the women would come up on the house-tops and the bells would ring in the temples. But as he attempted to follow with his eye the turns of the streets, the Englishman saw that they died out in wood tangle and blocks of fallen stone, and that some of the houses were rent with great cracks, and pierced from roof to road with holes that let in the morning sun. The drip-stones of the eaves were gap-toothed, and the tracery of the screens had fallen out so that zenana-rooms lay shamelessly open to the day. On the outskirts of the city, the strong walled houses dwindled and sank down to mere stone-heaps and faint indications of plinth and wall, hard to trace against the background of stony soil. The shadow of the palace lay over two-thirds of the city and the trees deepened the shadow. "He who has bent him o'er the dead" *after* the hour of which Byron sings, knows that the features of the man become blunted as it were—the face begins to fade. The same hideous look lies on the face of the Queen of the Pass, and when once this is realised, the eye wonders that it could have ever believed in the life of her. She is the city "whose graves are set in the side of the pit, and her company is, round about here graves," sister of Pathros, Zoan and No.

Moved by a thoroughly insular instinct, the Englishman took up a piece of plaster and heaved it from the palace wall into the dark streets below. It bounded from a house-top to a window-ledge, and thence into a little square, and the sound of its fall was hollow and echoing, as the sound of a stone in a well. Then the silence closed up upon the sound, till in the far away courtyard below the roped stallions began screaming afresh. There may be desolation in the great Indian Desert to the westward, and there is desolation upon the open seas; but the desolation of Amber is beyond the loneliness either of land or sea. Men by the hundred thousand must have toiled at the walls that bound it, the temples and bastions that stud the walls, the fort that overlooks all, the canals that once lifted water to the palace, and the garden in the lake of the valley. Renan could describe it as it stands to-day, and Vereschagin could paint it.

Arrived at this satisfactory conclusion, the Englishman went down through the palace and the scores of venomous and suggestive little rooms to the elephant in the courtyard and was taken back in due time to the Nineteenth Century in the shape of His Highness the Maharaja's Cotton Press, returning a profit of 27 per cent., and fitted with two engines of fifty horse-power each, an hydraulic press capable of exerting a pressure of three tons per square inch, and everything else to correspond. It stood under a neat corrugated iron roof close to the Jeypore Railway Station, and was in most perfect order, but somehow it did not taste well after Amber. There was aggressiveness about the engines and the smell of the raw cotton.

The modern side of Jeypore must not be mixed with the ancient.

IV.

The Temple of Mahadeo and the Manners of such as see India—The Man by the Water-Troughs and his Knowledge—The Voice of the City and what it said—Personalities and the Hospital—The House Beautiful of Jeypore and its Builders.

FROM the Cotton Press the Englishman wandered through the wide streets till he came into a Hindu Temple—rich in marble, stone and inlay, and a deep and tranquil silence, close to the Public Library of the State. The brazen bull was hung with flowers, and men were burning the evening incense before Mahadeo, while those who had prayed their prayer, beat upon the bells hanging from the roof and passed out, secure in the knowledge that the god had heard them. If there be much religion, there is little reverence, as Westerns understand the term, in the services of the gods of the East. A tiny little maiden, child of a monstrously ugly priest with one chalk-white eye, staggered across the marble pavement to the shrine and threw, with a gust of childish laughter, the blossoms she was carrying into the lap of the great Mahadeo himself. Then she made as though she would leap up to the bells and ran away, still laughing, into the shadow of the cells behind the shrine, while her father explained that she was but a baby and that Mahadeo would take no notice. The temple, he said, was specially favored by the Maharaja, and drew from lands an income of twenty thousand rupees a year. Thakoors and great men also gave gifts out of their benevolence; and there was nothing in the wide world to prevent an Englishman from following their example.

By this time, for Amber and the Cotton Press had filled the hours, night was falling, and the priests unhooked the swinging jets and began to light up the impassive face of Mahadeo with gas! They used Tændstikker matches.

Full night brought the hotel and its curiously-composed human menagerie.

There is, if a work-a-day world will give credit, a society entirely outside, and unconnected with, that of the Station—a planet within a planet, where nobody knows anything about the Collector's wife, the Colonel's dinner-party, or what was really the matter with the Engineer. It is a curious, an insatiably curious, thing, and its literature is Newman's *Bradshaw*.

Wandering "old arms-sellers" and others live upon it, and so do the garnetmen and the makers of ancient Rajput shields. The world of the innocents abroad is a touching and unsophisticated place, and its very atmosphere urges the Anglo-Indian unconsciously to extravagant mendacity. Can you wonder, then, that a guide of long-standing should in time grow to be an accomplished liar?

Into this world sometimes breaks the Anglo-Indian returned from leave, or a fugitive to the sea, and his presence is like that of a well-known landmark in the desert. The old arms-seller knows and avoids him, and he is detested by the jobber of gharis who calls everyone "my lord" in English, and panders to the "glaring race anomaly" by saying that every carriage not under his control is "rotten, my lord, having been used by natives." One of the privileges of playing at tourist is the brevet-rank of "Lord." *Hazur* is not to be compared with it.

There are many, and some very curious, methods of seeing India. One of these is buying English translations of the more Zolaistic of Zola's novels and reading them from breakfast to dinner-time in the verandah. Yet another, even simpler, is American in its conception. Take a Newman's *Bradshaw* and a blue pencil, and race up and down the length of the Empire, ticking off the names of the stations "done." To do this thoroughly, keep strictly to the railway buildings and form your conclusions through the carriage-windows. These eyes have seen both ways of working in full blast and, on the whole, the first is the most commendable.

Let us consider now with due reverence the modern side of Jeypore. It is difficult to write of a nickel-plated civilisation set down under the immemorial Aravalis in the first state of Rajputana. The red-grey hills seem to laugh at it, and the ever-shifting sand-dunes under the hills take no account of it, for they advance upon the bases of the monogrammed, coronet-crowned lamp-posts, and fill up the points of the natty tramways near the Water-works, which are the outposts of the civilisation of Jeypore.

Escape from the city by the Railway Station till you meet the cactus and the mud-bank and the Maharaja's Cotton Press. Pass between a tramway and a trough for wayfaring camels till your foot sinks ankle-deep in soft sand, and you come upon what seems to be the fringe of illimitable desert—mound upon mound of tussocks overgrown with plumed grass where the parrots sit and swing. Here, if you have kept to the road, you shall find a bund faced with stone, a great tank, and pumping machinery fine as the heart of a municipal engineer can desire—pure water, sound pipes and well-kept engines. If you belong to what is sarcastically styled an "able and intelligent municipality" under the British Raj, go down to the level of the tank, scoop up the water in your hands and drink, thinking meanwhile of the defects of the town whence you came. The experience will be a profitable one. There are statistics in connection with the Water-works, figures relating to "three-throw-plungers," delivery and supply, which should be known to the professional reader. They would not interest the unprofessional who would learn his lesson among the thronged stand-pipes of the city.

While the Englishman was preparing in his mind a scathing rebuke for an erring municipality that he knew of, a camel swung across the sands, its driver's jaw and brow bound mummy fashion to guard against the dust. The man was evidently a stranger to the place, for he pulled up and asked the Englishman where the drinking troughs were. He was a gentleman and bore very patiently with the Englishman's absurd ignorance of his dialect. He had come from some village, with an unpronounceable name, thirty *kos* away, to see his brother's son who was sick in the big Hospital. While the camel was drinking, the man talked, lying back on his mount. He knew nothing of Jeypore, except the names of certain Englishmen in it, the men who, he said, had made the Water-works and built the Hospital for his brother's son's comfort.

And this is the curious feature of Jeypore; though happily the city is not unique in its peculiarity. When the late Maharaja ascended the throne, more than fifty years ago, it was his royal will and pleasure that Jeypore should advance. Whether he was prompted by love for his subjects, desire for praise, or the magnificent vanity with which Jey Singh must have been so largely dowered, are questions that concern nobody. In the latter years of his reign, he was supplied with Englishmen who made the State their father-land, and identified themselves with its progress as only Englishmen can. Behind them stood the Maharaja ready to spend money with a lavishness that no Supreme Government would dream of; and it would not be too much to say that the two made the State what it is. When Ram Singh died, Madho Singh, his successor, a conservative Hindu, forebore to interfere in any way with the work that was going forward. It is said in the city that he does not overburden himself with the cares of State, the driving power being mainly in the hands of a Bengali, who has everything but the name of Minister. Nor do the Englishmen, it is said in the city, mix themselves with the business of Government; their business being wholly executive.

They can, according to the voice of the city, do what they please, and the voice of the city—not in the main roads but in the little side-alleys where the stall-less bull blocks the path—attests how well their pleasure has suited the pleasure of the people. In truth, to men of action few things could be more delightful than having a State of fifteen thousand square miles placed at their disposal, as it were, to leave their mark on. Unfortunately for the vagrant traveller, those who work hard for practical ends prefer not to talk about their doings, and he must, therefore, pick up what information he can at second-hand or in the city. The men at the stand-pipes explain that the Maharaja Sahib's father gave the order for the Water-works and that Yakub Sahib made them—not only in the city but out away in the district. "Did people grow more crops thereby?" "Of course they did: were canals made to wash in only?" "How much more crops?" "Who knows. The Sahib had better go and ask some official." Increased irrigation means increase of revenue for the State somewhere, but the man who brought about the increase does not say so.

After a few days of amateur globe-trotting, a shamelessness great as that of the other loafer—the red-nosed man who hangs about compounds and is always on the eve of starting for Calcutta—possesses the masquerader; so that he feels equal to asking a Resident for a parcel-gilt howdah, or dropping in to dinner with a Lieutenant-Governor. No man has a right to keep anything back from a Globe-Trotter, who is a mild, temperate, gentlemanly and unobtrusive seeker after truth. Therefore he who, without a word of enlightenment, sends the visitor into a city which he himself has beautified and adorned and made clean and wholesome, deserves unsparing exposure. And the city may be trusted to betray him. The *malli* in the Ram Newa's Gardens, gardens—here the Englishman can speak from a fairly extensive experience—finer than any in India and fit to rank with the best in Paris—says that the Maharaja gave the order and Yakub Sahib made the Gardens. He also says that the Hospital just outside the Gardens was built by Yakub Sahib, and if the Sahib will go to the centre of the

Gardens, he will find another big building, a Museum by the same hand.

But the Englishman went first to the Hospital, and found the out-patients beginning to arrive. A hospital cannot tell lies about its own progress as a municipality can. Sick folk either come or lie in their own villages. In the case of the Mayo Hospital they came, and the operation-book showed that they had been in the habit of coming. Doctors at issue with provincial and local administrations, Civil Surgeons who cannot get their indents complied with, ground-down and mutinous practitioners all India over, would do well to visit the Mayo Hospital, Jeypore. They might, in the exceeding bitterness of their envy, be able to point out some defects in its supplies, or its beds, or its splints, or in the absolute isolation of the women's quarters from the men's.

Envy is a low and degrading passion, and should be striven against. From the Hospital the Englishman went to the Museum in the centre of the Gardens, and was eaten up by it, for Museums appealed to him. The casing of the jewel was in the first place superb—a wonder of carven white stone of the Indo-Saracenic style. It stood on a stone plinth, and was rich in stone-tracery, green marble columns from Ajmir, red

Akbar's Palace.

marble, white marble colonnades, courts with fountains, richly-carved wooden doors, frescoes, inlay and colour. The ornamentation of the tombs of Delhi, the palaces of Agra and the walls of Amber, have been laid under contribution to supply the designs in bracket, arch, and soffit; and stone-masons from the Jeypore School of Art have woven into the work the best that their hands could produce. The building in essence, if not in the fact of to-day, is the work of Freemasons. The men were allowed a certain scope in their choice of detail and the result........but it should be seen to be understood, as it stands in those Imperial Gardens. And observe, the man who had designed it, who had superintended its erection, had said no word to indicate that there was such a thing in the place, or that every foot of it, from the domes of the roof to the cool green chunam dadoes and the carving of the rims of the fountains in the courtyard, was worth studying! Round the arches of the great centre court are written in Sanskrit and Hindi, texts from the great Hindu writers of old, bearing on the beauty of wisdom and the sanctity of knowledge.

In the central corridor are six great frescoes, each about nine feet by five, copies of illustrations in the Royal Folio of the *Razmnameh,* the

Mahabharata, which Akbar caused to be done by the best artists of his day. The original is in the Museum, and he who can steal it, will find a purchaser at any price up to fifty thousand pounds.

V.

Of the Sordidness of the Supreme Government on the Revenue Side; and of the Palace of Jeypore—A great King's Pleasure-House, and the Work of the Servants of State.

INTERNALLY, there is, in all honesty, no limit to the luxury of the Jeypore Museum. It revels in "South Kensington" cases— of the approved pattern—that turn the beholder home-sick, and South Kensington labels, whereon the description, measurements and price of each object, are fairly printed. These make savage one who knows how labelling is bungled in some of the Government Museums—those starved barns that are supposed to hold the economic exhibits, not of little States but of great Provinces.

The floors are of dark red chunam, overlaid with a discreet and silent matting; the doors, where they are not plate-glass, are of carved wood, no two alike, hinged by sumptuous brass hinges on to marble jambs and opening without noise. On the carved marble pillars of each hall are fixed revolving cases of the S. K. M.

pattern to show textile fabrics, gold lace and the like. In the recesses of the walls are more cases, and on the railing of the gallery that runs round each of the three great central rooms, are fixed low cases to hold natural history specimens and models of fruits and vegetables.

Hear this, Governments of India from the Punjab to Madras! The doors come true to the jamb, the cases, which have been through a hot weather, are neither warped nor cracked, nor are there unseemly tallow-drops and flaws in the glasses. The maroon cloth, on or against which the exhibits are placed, is of close texture, untouched by the moth, neither stained nor meagre nor sunfaded; the revolving cases revolve freely and without rattling; there is not a speck of dust from one end of the building to the other, because the menial staff are numerous enough to keep everything clean, and the Curator's office is a veritable office—not a shed or a bath-room, or a loose-box partitioned from the main building. These things are so because money has been spent on the Museum, and it is now a rebuke to all other Museums in India, from Calcutta downwards. Whether it is not too good to be buried away in a Native State is a question which envious men may raise and answer as they choose. Not long ago, the Editor of a

Bombay paper passed through it, but having the interests of the Egocentric Presidency before his eyes, dwelt more upon the idea of the building than its structural beauties; saying that Bombay, who professed a weakness for technical education, should be ashamed of herself. And herein he was quite right.

The system of the Museum is complete in intention as are its appointments in design. At present there are some fifteen thousand objects of art, "surprising in themselves" as, Count Smaltork would say, a complete exposition of the arts, from enamels to pottery and from brassware to stone-carving, of the State of Jeypore. They are compared with similar arts of other lands. Thus a Damio's sword—a gem of lacquer-plaited silk and stud-work—flanks the *tulwars* of Marwar and the *jezails* of Tonk; and reproductions of Persian and Russian brasswork stand side by side with the handicrafts of the pupils of the Jeypore School of Art. A photograph of His Highness the present Maharaja is set among the arms, which are the most prominent features of the first or metal-room. As the villagers enter, they salaam reverently to the photo, and then move on slowly, with an evidently intelligent interest in what they see. Ruskin could describe the scene admirably—

pointing out how reverence must precede the study of art, and how it is good for Englishmen and Rajputs alike to bow on occasion before Gessler's cap. They thumb the revolving cases of cloths do these rustics, and artlessly try to feel the texture through the protecting glass. The main object of the Museum is avowedly provincial—to show the craftsman of Jeypore the best that his predecessors could do, and to show him what foreign artists have done. In time—but the Curator of the Museum has many schemes which will assuredly bear fruit in time, and it would be unfair to divulge them. Let those who doubt the thoroughness of a Museum under one man's control, built, filled, and endowed with royal generosity—an institution perfectly independent of the Government of India—go and exhaustively visit Dr. Hendley's charge at Jeypore. Like the man who made the building, he refuses to talk, and so the greater part of the work that he has in hand must be guessed at.

At one point, indeed, the Curator was taken off his guard. A huge map of the kingdom showed in green the portions that had been brought under irrigation, while blue circles marked the towns that owned dispensaries. "I want to bring every man in the State within twenty miles of a dispensary, and I've nearly done it," said he. Then he checked himself, and went off to food-grains in little bottles as being neutral and colourless things. Envy is forced to admit that the arrangement of the Museum—far too important a matter to be explained off-hand—is Continental in its character, and has a definite end and bearing—a trifle omitted by many institutions other than Museums. But—in fine, what can one say of a collection whose very labels are gilt-edged! Shameful extravagance? Nothing of the kind—only finish, perfectly in keeping with the rest of the fittings—a finish that we in *kutcha* India have failed to catch. That is all!

From the Museum go out through the city to the Maharaja's Palace—skilfully avoiding the man who would show you the Maharaja's European billiard-room, and wander through a wilderness of sunlit, sleepy courts, gay with paint and frescoes, till you reach an inner square, where smiling grey-bearded men squat at ease and play *chaupur*—just such a game as cost the Pandavs the fair Draupadi—with inlaid dice and gaily lacquered pieces. These ancients are very polite and will press you to play, but give no heed to them, for *chaupur* is an expensive game—expensive as quail-fighting, when you have backed the wrong bird and the people are laughing at your inexperience. The Maharaja's Palace is arrogantly gay, overwhelmingly rich in candelabra, painted ceilings, gilt mirrors and other evidences of a too hastily assimilated civilisation; but, if the evidence of the ear can be trusted, the old, old game of intrigue goes on as merrily as of yore. A figure in saffron came out of a dark arch into the sunlight, almost falling into the arms of one in pink. "Where have you come from?" "I have been to see——"the name was unintelligible. "That is a lie: you have *not!*" Then, across the court, some one laughed a low croaking laugh. The pink and saffron figures separated as though they had been shot, and disappeared into separate bolt-holes. It was a curious little incident, and might have meant a great deal or just nothing at all. It distracted the attention of the ancients bowed above the *chaupur* cloth.

In the Palace-gardens there is even a greater stillness than that about the courts, and here nothing of the West, unless a hypercritical soul might take exception to the lamp-posts. At the extreme end lies a lake-like tank swarming with *muggers*. It is reached through an opening under a block of zenana buildings. Remembering that all beasts by the palaces of Kings or the temples of priests in this country would answer to the name of "Brother," the Englishman cried with the voice of faith across the water, in a key as near as might be to the melodious howl of the "monkey faquir" on the top of Jakko. And the mysterious freemasonry did not fail. At the far end of the tank rose a ripple that grew and grew and grew like a thing in a nightmare, and became presently an aged *mugger*. As he neared the shore, there emerged, the green slime thick upon his eyelids, another beast, and the two together snapped at a cigar-butt—the only reward for their courtesy. Then, disgusted, they sank stern first with a gentle sigh. Now a *mugger's* sigh is the most suggestive sound in animal speech. It suggested first the zenana buildings overhead, the walled passes through the purple hills beyond, a horse that might clatter through the passes till he reached the Man Sagar Lake below the passes, and a boat that might row across the Man Sagar till it nosed the wall of the Palace-tank and then—then uprose the *mugger* with the filth upon his forehead and winked one horny eyelid—in truth he did!—and so supplied a fitting end to a foolish fiction of old days and things that might have been. But it must be unpleasant to live in a house whose base is washed by such a tank.

And so back as Pepys says, through the chu-

named courts, and among the gentle sloping paths between the orange trees, up to an entrance of the Palace guarded by two rusty brown dogs from Kabul, each big as a man, and each requiring a man's charpoy to sleep upon. Very gay was the front of the Palace, very brilliant were the glimpses of the damask-couched, gilded rooms within, and very, very civilised were the lamp-posts with Ram Singh's monogram, devised to look like V. R., at the bottom, and a coronet, as hath been shown, at the top. An unseen brass band among the orange-bushes struck up the overture of the *Bronze Horse*. Those who know the music will see at once that that was the only tune which exactly and perfectly fitted the scene and its surroundings. It was a coincidence and a revelation.

In his time and when he was not fighting, Jey Singh the Second, who built the city, was a great astronomer—a royal Omar Khayyam, for he, like the tent-maker of Nishapur, reformed a calendar, and strove to wring their mysteries from the stars with instruments worthy of a King. But in the end he wrote that the goodness of the Almighty was above everything, and died; leaving his observatory to decay without the Palace-grounds.

From the *Bronze Horse* to the grass-grown

enclosure that holds the Yantr Samrat, or Prince of Dials, is rather an abrupt passage. Jey Singh built him a dial with a gnomon some ninety feet high, to throw a shadow against the sun, and the gnomon stands to-day, though there is grass in the kiosque at the top and the flight of steps up the hypotenuse is worn. He built also a zodiacal dial—twelve dials upon one platform—to find the moment of true noon at any time of the year, and hollowed out of the earth place for two hemispherical cups, cut by belts of stone, for comparative observations.

He made cups for calculating eclipses, and a mural quadrant and many other strange things of stone and mortar, of which people hardly know the names and but very little of the uses. Once, said the keeper of two tiny elephants, *Indur* and *Har*, a *Sahib* came with the *Burra Lat Sahib*, and spent eight days in the enclosure of the great neglected observatory, seeing and writing things in a book. But *he* understood Sanskrit—the Sanskrit upon the faces of the dials, and the meaning of the gnoma and pointers. Now-a-days no one understands Sanskrit—not even the Pundits; but without doubt Jey Singh was a great man.

The hearer echoed the statement, though he knew nothing of astronomy, and of all the wonders in the observatory was only struck by the fact that the shadow of the Prince of Dials moved over its vast plate so quickly that it seemed as though Time, wroth at the insolence of Jey Singh, had loosed the Horses of the Sun and were sweeping everything—dainty Palace-gardens and ruinous instruments—into the darkness of eternal night. So he went away chased by the shadow on the dial, and returned to the hotel, where he found men who said—this must be a catch-word of Globe-Trotters—that they were "much pleased at" Amber. They further thought that "house-rent would be cheap in those parts," and sniggered over the witticism. Jey Singh, in spite of a few discreditable *laches,* was a temperate and tolerant man; but he would have hanged those Globe-Trotters in their trunk-straps as high as the Yantr Samrat.

Next morning, in the grey dawn, the Englishman rose up and shook the sand of Jeypore from his feet, and went with Master Coryatt and Sir Thomas Roe to "Adsmir," wondering whether a year in Jeypore would be sufficient to exhaust its interest, and why he had not gone out to the tombs of the dead Kings and the passes of Gulta and the fort of Motee Dungri. But what he wondered at most—knowing how many men who have in any way been connected with the birth of an institution, do, to the end of their days, continue to drag forward and exhume their labours and the honours that did *not* come to them—was the work of the two men who, together for years past, have been pushing Jeypore along the stone-dressed paths of civilisation, peace and comfort. "Servants of the Raj" they called themselves, and surely they have served the Raj past all praise. The pen and tact of a Wilfred Blunt are needed to fitly lash their reticence. But the people in the city and the camel-driver from the sand-hills told of them. They themselves held their peace as to what they had done, and, when pressed, referred —crowning baseness—to reports. Printed ones!

VI.

Showing how Her Majesty's Mails went to Udaipur and fell out by the Way.

ARRIVED at Ajmir, the Englishman fell among tents pitched under the shadow of a huge banian tree, and in them was a Punjabi. Now there is no brotherhood like the brotherhood of the Pauper Province; for it is even greater than the genial and unquestioning hospitality which, in spite of the loafer and the Globe-Trotter, seems to exist throughout India. Ajmir being British territory, though the inhabitants are allowed to carry arms, is the headquarters of many of the banking firms who lend to the Native States. The complaint of the Setts to-day is that their trade is bad, because an unsympathetic Government induces the Native States to make railways and become prosperous. "Look at Jodhpur!" said a gentleman whose possessions might be roughly estimated at anything between thirty and forty-five lakhs. "Time was when Jodhpur was always in debt—and not so long ago, either. Now, they've got a railroad and are carrying salt over it, and, as sure as I stand here, they have a *surplus!* What can we do?" Poor pauper! However, he makes a little profit on the fluctuations in the coinage of the States round him, for every small king seems to have the privilege of striking his own image and inflicting the Great Exchange Question on his subjects. It is a poor State that has not two seers and five different rupees.

From a criminal point of view, Ajmir is not a pleasant place. The Native States lie all round and about it, and portions of the district are ten miles off, Native State-locked on every side. Thus the criminal, who may be a burglarious Meena lusting for the money bags of the Setts, or a Peshawari down south on a cold weather tour, has his plan of campaign much simplified. The Englishman made only a short stay in the town, hearing that there was to be a ceremony—*tamasha* covers a multitude of things—at the capital of His Highness the Maharana of Udaipur—a town some hundred and eighty miles south of Ajmir, not known to many people beyond Viceroys and their Staffs and the officials of the Rajputana Agency. So he took a Neemuch train in the very early morning and, with the Punjabi, went due south to Chitor, the point of departure for Udaipur. In time the Aravalis gave place to a dead, flat, stone-strewn plain, thick with dhak-jungle.

Later the date-palm fraternised with the dhak, and low hills stood on either side of the line. To this succeeded a tract rich in pure white stone, the line was ballasted with it. Then came more low hills, each with comb of splintered rock a-top, overlooking dhak-jungle and villages fenced with thorns—places that at once declared themselves tigerish. Last, the huge bulk of Chitor showed itself on the horizon. The train crossed the Gumber River and halted almost in the shadow of the hills on which the old pride of Udaipur was set.

It is difficult to give an idea of the Chitor fortress; but the long line of brown wall springing out of bush-covered hill suggested at once those pictures, such as the *Graphic* publishes, of the *Inflexible* or the *Devastation*—gigantic men-of-war with a very low free-board ploughing through green sea. The hill on which the fort stands is ship-shaped and some miles long, and, from a distance, every inch appears to be scarped and guarded. But there was no time to see Chitor. The business of the day was to get, if possible, to Udaipur from Chitor Station, which was composed of one platform, one telegraph-room, a bench and several vicious dogs.

The State of Udaipur is as backward as Jeypore is advanced—if we judge it by the standard of civilisation. It does not approve of the incursions of Englishmen, and, to do it justice, it thoroughly succeeds in conveying its silent sulkiness. Still, where there is one English Resident, one Doctor, one Engineer, one Settlement Officer and one Missionary, there must be a mail at least once a day. There was a mail. The Englishman, men said, might go by it if he liked, or he might not. Then, with a great sinking of the heart, he began to realise that his caste was of no value in the stony pastures of Mewar, among the swaggering gentlemen who were so lavishly adorned with arms. There was a mail, the ghost of a tonga, with tattered side-cloths and patched roof, inconceivably filthy within and without, and it was Her Majesty's. There was another tonga—an *aram* tonga—but the Englishman was not to have it. It was reserved for a Rajput Thakur who was going to Udaipur with his "tail." The Thakur, in claret-coloured velvet with a blue turban, a revolver—Army pattern—a sword, and five or six friends, also with swords, came by and endorsed the statement. Now, the mail tonga had a wheel which was destined to become the Wheel of Fate, and to lead to many curious things. Two diseased yellow ponies were extracted from a dung-hill and yoked to the tonga; and after due deliberation Her Majesty's mail started, the Thakur following.

In twelve hours, or thereabouts, the seventy miles between Chitor and Udaipur would be accomplished. Behind the tonga cantered an armed sowar. He was the guard. The Thakur's tonga came up with a rush, ran deliberately across the bows of the Englishman, shipped a pony, and passed on. One lives and learns. The Thakur seems to object to following the foreigner.

At the halting-stages, once in every six miles, that is to say, the ponies were carefully undressed and all their accoutrements fitted more or less accurately on to the backs of the ponies that might happen to be near: the released animals finding their way back to their stables alone and unguided. There were no *syces*, and the harness hung on by special dispensation of Providence. Still the ride over a good road, driven through a pitilessly stony country, had its charms for a while. At sunset the low hills turned to opal and wine-red, and the brown dust flew up pure gold; for the tonga was running straight into the sinking sun. Now and again would pass a traveller on a camel, or a gang of *Bunjarras* with their pack-bullocks and their women; and the sun touched the brasses of their swords and guns till the poor wretches seemed rich merchants come back from travelling with Sindbad.

On a rock on the right hand side, thirty-four great vultures were gathered over the carcase of a steer. And this was an evil omen. They made unseemly noises as the tonga passed, and a raven came out of a bush on the right and answered them. To crown all, one of the hide and skin castes sat on the left hand side of the road, cutting up some of the flesh that he had stolen from the vultures. Could a man desire three more inauspicious signs for a night's travel? Twilight came, and the hills were alive with strange noises, as the red moon, nearly at her full, rose over Chitor. To the low hills of the mad geological formation, the tumbled strata that seem to obey no law, succeeded level ground, the pasture lands of Mewar, cut by the Beruch and Wyan, streams running over smooth water-worn rock, and, as the heavy embankments and ample waterways showed, very lively in the rainy season.

In this region occurred the last and most inauspicious omen of all. Something had gone wrong with a crupper, a piece of blue and white punkah-cord. The Englishman pointed it out, and the driver, descending, danced on that lonely road an unholy dance, singing the while:—

"The *dumchi!* The *dumchi!* The *dumchi!*" in a shrill voice. Then he returned and drove on, while the Englishman wondered into what land of lunatics he was heading. At an average speed of six miles an hour, it is possible to see a great deal of the country; and, under brilliant moonlight, Mewar was desolately beautiful. There was no night traffic on the road—no one except the patient sowar, his shadow an inky blot on white, cantering twenty yards behind. Once the tonga strayed into a company of date-trees that fringed the path, and once rattled through a little town, and once the ponies shyed at what the driver said was a rock; but it jumped up in the moonlight and went away.

Then came a great blasted heath whereon nothing was more than six inches high—a wilderness covered with grass and low thorn; and here, as nearly as might be midway between Chitor and Udaipur, the Wheel of Fate, which had been for some time beating against the side of the tonga, came off, and Her Majesty's Mails, two bags including parcels, collapsed on the way side; while the Englishman repented him that he had neglected the omens of the vultures and the raven, the low caste man and the mad driver.

There was a consultation and an examination of the wheel; but the whole tonga was rotten, and the axle was smashed and the axle-pins were bent and nearly red-hot. "It is nothing," said the driver, "the mail often does this. What is a wheel?" He took a big stone and began hammering the wheel proudly on the tyre, to show that that at least was sound. A hasty court-martial revealed that there was absolutely not one single "breakdown tonga" on the whole road between Chitor and Udaipur.

Now this wilderness was so utterly waste that not even the barking of a dog or the sound of a nightfowl could be heard. Luckily the Thakur had, some twenty miles back, stepped out to smoke by the roadside, and his tonga had been passed meanwhile. The sowar was sent back to find that tonga and bring it on. He cantered into the haze of the moonlight and disappeared. Then said the driver:—"Had there been no tonga behind us, I should have put the mails on a horse, because the Sirkar's dak cannot stop." The Englishman sat down upon the parcels-bag, for he felt that there was trouble coming. The driver looked East and West and said:—"I too will go and see if the tonga can be found, for the Sirkar's dak cannot stop. Meantime, Oh Sahib, do you take care of the mails—one bag and one bag of parcels." So he ran swiftly into the haze of the moonlight and was lost, and the

Englishman was left alone in charge of Her Majesty's Mails, two unhappy ponies and a lop-sided tonga. He lit fires, for the night was bitterly cold, and only mourned that he could not destroy the whole of the territories of His Highness the Maharana of Udaipur. But he managed to raise a very fine blaze, before he reflected that all this trouble was his own fault for wandering into Native States undesirous of Englishmen.

The ponies coughed dolorously from time to time, but they could not lift the weight of a dead silence that seemed to be crushing the earth. After an interval measurable by centuries, sowar, driver and Thakur's tonga reappeared; the latter full to the brim and bubbling over with humanity and bedding. "We will now," said the driver, not deigning to notice the Englishman who had been on guard over the mails, "put the Sirkar's dak into this tonga and go forward." Amiable heathen! He was going, he said so, to leave the Englishman to wait in the Sahara, for certainly thirty hours and perhaps forty-eight. Tongas are scarce on the Udaipur road. There are a few occasions in life when it is justifiable to delay Her Majesty's Mails. This was one of them. Seating himself upon the parcels-bag, the Englishman cried in what was intended to be a very terrible voice, but the silence soaked it up and left only a thin trickle of sound, that any one who touched the bags would be hit with a stick, several times, over the head. The bags were the only link between him and the civilisation he had so rashly foregone. And there was a pause.

The Thakur put his head out of the tonga and spoke shrilly in Mewari. The Englishman replied in English-Urdu. The Thakur withdrew his head, and from certain grunts that followed seemed to be wakening his retainers. Then two men fell sleepily out of the tonga and walked into the night. "Come in," said the Thakur, "you and your baggage. My *banduq* is in that corner; be careful." The Englishman, taking a mail-bag in one hand for safety's sake—the wilderness inspires an Anglo-Indian Cockney with unreasoning fear—climbed into the tonga, which was then loaded far beyond Plimsoll mark, and the procession resumed its journey. Every one in the vehicle,—it seemed as full as the railway carriage that held Alice. Through the Looking Glass—was *Sahib* and *Hazur*. Except the Englishman. He was simple *tum,* and a revolver, Army pattern, was printing every diamond in the chequer-work of its handle, into his right hip. When men desired him to move, they prodded him with the handles of *tulwars* till they had coiled him into an uneasy lump. Then they slept upon him, or cannoned against him as the tonga bumped. It was an *aram* tonga or tonga for ease. That was the bitterest thought of all.

In due season the harness began to break once every five minutes, and the driver vowed that the wheels would give way also.

After eight hours in one position, it is excessively difficult to walk, still more difficult to climb up an unknown road into a dak-bungalow; but he who has sought sleep on an arsenal and under the bodies of burly Rajputs, can do it. The grey dawn brought Udaipur and a French bedstead. As the tonga jingled away, the Englishman heard the familiar crack of broken harness. So he was not the Jonah he had been taught to consider himself all through that night of penance!

A jackal sat in the verandah and howled him to sleep, wherein he dreamed that he had caught a Viceroy under the walls of Chitor and beaten him with a *tulwar* till he turned into a dak-pony whose near foreleg was perpetually coming off, and who would say nothing but *um* when he was asked why he had not built a railway from Chitor to Udaipur.

VII.

Touching the Children of the Sun and their City, and the Hat-marked Caste and their Merits, and a Good Man's Works in the Wilderness.

IT was worth a night's discomfort and a revolver-bed to sleep upon—this city of the Suryavansi, hidden among the hills that encompass the great Pichola lake. Truly, the King who governs to-day is wise in his determination to have no railroad to his capital. His predecessor was more or less enlightened, and had he lived a few years longer, would have brought the iron horse through the Dobarri—the green gate which is the entrance of the Girwa or girdle of hills round Udaipur; and, with the train, would have come the tourist who would have scratched his name upon the Temple of Garuda and laughed horse-laughs upon the lake. Let us, therefore, be thankful that the capital of Mewar is hard to reach, and go abroad into a new and a strange land rejoicing.

Each man who has any claims to respectability walks armed, carrying his tulwar sheathed in his hand, or hung by a short sling of cotton passing over the shoulder, under his left armpit. His matchlock, or smooth-bore if he has one, is borne naked on the shoulder.

Now it is possible to carry any number of lethal weapons without being actually dangerous. An unhandy revolver, for instance, may be worn for years, and, at the end, accomplish nothing more noteworthy than the murder of its owner. But the Rajput's weapons are not meant for display. The Englishman caught a camel-driver who talked to him in Mewari, which is a heathenish dialect, something like Multani to listen to; and the man, very gracefully and courteously, handed him his sword and matchlock, the latter a heavy stump-stock arrangement without pretence of sights. The blade was as sharp as a razor, and the gun in perfect working order. The coiled fuse on the stock was charred at the end, and the curled ram's-horn powder-horn opened as readily as a whisky-flask that is much handled. Unfortunately, ignorance of Mewari prevented conversation; so the camel-driver resumed his accoutrements and jogged forward on his beast—a superb black one, with the short curled *hubshee* hair—while the Englishman went to the City, which is built on hills on the borders of

Street Scene 'n Udaipur.

the lake. By the way, everything in Udaipur is built on a hill. There is no level ground in the place, except the Durbar Gardens, of which more hereafter. Because colour holds the eye more than form, the first thing noticeable was neither temple nor fort, but an ever-recurring picture, painted in the rudest form of native art, of a man on horseback armed with a lance, charging an elephant-of-war. As a rule, the elephant was depicted on one side the house-door and the rider on the other. There was no representation of an army behind. The figures stood alone upon the whitewash on house and wall and gate, again and again and again. A highly intelligent priest grunted that it was a *tazwir;* a private of the Maharana's regular army suggested that it was a *hathi;* while a wheat-seller, his sword at his side, was equally certain that it was a Raja. Beyond that point, his knowledge did not go. The explanation of the picture is this. In the days when Raja Maun of Amber put his sword at Akbar's sevice and won for him great kingdoms, Akbar sent an army against Mewar, whose then ruler was Pertap Singh, most famous of all the princes of Mewar. Selim, Akbar's son, led the army of the Toork; the Rajputs met them at the pass of Huldighat and fought till one-half of their bands were slain. Once, in the press of battle, Pertap, on his great horse, "Chytak," came within striking distance of Selim's elephant, and slew the *mahout,* but Selim escaped, to become Jehangir afterwards, and the Rajputs were broken. That was three hundred years ago, and men have reduced the picture to a sort of diagram that the painter dashes in, in a few minutes, without, it would seem, knowing what he is commemorating. Elsewhere, the story is drawn in line even more roughly.

Thinking of these things, the Englishman made shift to get at the City, and presently came to a tall gate, the gate of the Sun, on which the elephant-spikes, that he had seen rotted with rust at Amber, were new and pointed and effective. The City gates are said to be shut at night, and there is a story of a Viceroy's Guard-of-Honour which arrived before daybreak, being compelled to crawl ignominiously man by man through a little wicket gate, while the horses had to wait without till sunrise. But a civilised yearning for the utmost advantages of octroi, and not a fierce fear of robbery and wrong, is at the bottom of the continuance of this custom. The walls of the City are loopholed for musketry, but there seem to be no mountings for guns, and the moat without the walls is dry and gives cattle pasture. Coarse rubble in concrete faced with stone, makes the walls moderately strong.

Internally, the City is surprisingly clean, though with the exception of the main street, paved after the fashion of Jullundur, of which, men say, the pavement was put down in the time of Alexander and worn by myriads of naked feet into deep barrels and grooves. In the case of Udaipur, the feet of the passengers have worn the rock veins that crop out everywhere, smooth and shiny; and in the rains the narrow gullies must spout like fire-hoses. The people have been untouched by cholera for four years—proof that Providence looks after those who do not look after themselves, for Neemuch Cantonment, a hundred miles away, suffered grievously last summer. "And what do you make in Udaipur?" "Swords," said the man in the shop, throwing down an armful of *tulwars, kuttars* and *khandas* on the stones. "Do you want any? Look here!" Hereat, he took up one of the commoner swords and flourished it in the sunshine. Then he bent it double, and, as it sprang straight, began to make it "speak." Arm-vendors in Udaipur are a genuine race, for they sell to people who really use their wares. The man in the shop was rude—distinctly so. His first flush of professional enthusiasm abated, he took stock of the Englishman and said calmly:—"What do *you* want with a sword?" Then he picked up his goods and retreated, while certain small boys, who deserved a smacking, laughed riotously from the coping of a little temple hard by. Swords seem to be the sole manufacture of the place. At least, none of the inhabitants the Englishman spoke to could think of any other.

There is a certain amount of personal violence in and about the State, or else where would be the good of the weapons? There are occasionally dacoities more or less important; but these are not often heard of and, indeed, there is no special reason why they should be dragged into the light of an unholy publicity, for the land governs itself in its own way, and is always in its own way, which is by no means ours, very happy. The Thakurs live, each in his own castle on some rock-faced hill, much as they lived in the days of Tod; though their chances of distinguishing themselves, except in the school, sewer, and dispensary line, are strictly limited. Nominally, they pay *chutoond*, or a sixth of their revenues to the State, and are under feudal obligations to supply their Head with so many horsemen per thousand rupees; but whether the *chutoond* justifies its name and what is the exact extent of the "tail" leviable, they, and perhaps the Rajputana Agency, alone know. They are quiet, give no trouble except to the wild boar, and personally are magnificent men to look at. The Rajput shows his breeding in his hands and feet, which are almost disproportionately small, and as well shaped as those of women. His stirrups and sword-handles are even more unusable by Westerns than those elsewhere in India, while the Bhil's knife-handle gives as large a grip as an English one. Now the little Bhil is an aborigine which is humiliating to think of. His tongue, which may frequently be heard in the City, seems to possess some variant of the Zulu click; which gives it a weird and unearthly character. From the main gate of the City the Englishman climbed uphill towards the Palace and the Jugdesh Temple built by one Jaggat Singh at the beginning of the last century. This building must be—but ignorance is a bad guide—Jain in character. From basement to the stone socket of the temple flag-staff, it is carved in high relief with friezes of elephants, men, gods, and monsters in wearying profusion.

The management of the temple have daubed a large portion of the building with whitewash, for which their revenues should be "cut" for a year or two. The main shrine holds a large brazen image of Garuda, and, in the corners of the courtyard of the main pile, are shrines to Mahadeo, and the jovial, pot-bellied Ganesh. There is no repose in this architecture, and the entire effect is one of repulsion; for the clustered figures of man and brute seem always on the point of bursting into unclean, wriggling life. But it may be that the builders of this form of house desired to put the fear of all their many gods into the heart of the worshippers.

From the temple whose steps are worn smooth by the feet of men, and whose courts are full of the faint smell of stale flowers and old incense, the Englishman went to the Palaces which crown the highest hill overlooking the City. Here, too, whitewash had been unsparingly applied, but the excuse was that the stately fronts and the pierced screens were built of a perishable stone which needed protection against the weather. One projecting window in the facade of the main Palace has been treated with Minton tiles. Luckily it was too far up the wall for anything more than the colour to be visible, and the pale blue against the pure white was effective.

A picture of Ganesh looks out over the main courtyard which is entered by a triple gate, and hard by is the place where the King's elephants fight over a low masonry wall. In the side of the hill on which the Palaces stand, is built stabling for horses and elephants—proof that the architects of old must have understood their business thoroughly. The Palace is not a "show place," and, consequently, the Englishman did not see much of the interior. But he passed through open gardens with tanks and pavilions, very cool and restful, till he came suddenly upon the Pichola lake, and forgot altogether about the Palace. He found a sheet of steel-blue water, set in purple and grey hills, bound in, on one side, by marble bunds, the fair white walls of the Palace, and the grey, time-worn ones of the city; and, on the other, fading away through the white of shallow water, and the soft green of weed, marsh, and rank-pastured river field, into the land. To enjoy open water thoroughly, live for a certain number of years barred from anything better than the yearly swell and shrinkage of one of the Five Rivers, and then come upon two and a half miles of solid, restful lake, with a cool wind blowing off it and little waves spitting against the piers of a veritable, albeit hideously ugly, boat house. On the faith of an exile from the Sea, you will not stay long among Palaces, be they never so lovely, or in little rooms panelled with Dutch tiles, be these never so rare and curious. And here follows a digression. There is no life so good as the life of a loafer who travels by rail and road; for all things and all people are kind to him. From the chill miseries of a dak-bungalow where they slew one hen with as much parade as the French guillotined Pranzini, to the well-ordered sumptuousness of the Residency, was a step bridged over by kindly and unquestioning hospitality. So it happened that the Englishman was not only able to go upon the lake in a soft-cushioned boat, with everything handsome about him, but might, had he chosen, have killed wild-duck with which the lake swarms.

The mutter of water under a boat's nose was a pleasant thing to hear once more. Starting at the head of the lake, he found himself shut out from sight of the main sheet of water in a loch bounded by a sunk, broken bund to steer across which was a matter of some nicety. Beyond that lay a second pool spanned by a narrow-arched bridge built, men said, long before the City of the Rising Sun, which is little more than three hundred years old. The bridge connects the City with Brahmapura—a white-walled enclosure filled with many Brahmins and ringing with the noise of their conches. Beyond the bridge, the body of the lake, with the City running down to it, comes into full view; and Providence has arranged for the benefit of such as delight in colours, that the Rajputni shall wear the most striking tints that she can buy in the bazaars, in order that she may beautify the ghats where she comes to bathe.

The bathing-ledge at the foot of the City wall was lighted with women clad in raw vermilion, dull red, indigo and sky-blue, saffron and pink and turquoise; the water faithfully doubling everything. But the first impression was of the unreality of the sight, for the Englishman found himself thinking of the Simla Fine Arts Exhibition and the overdaring amateurs who had striven to reproduce scenes such as these. Then a woman rose up, and clasping her hands behind her head, looked at the passing boat, and the ripples spread out from her waist, in blinding white silver, far across the water. As a picture, a daringly insolent picture, it would have been superb.

The boat turned aside to shores where huge turtles were lying, and a stork had built her a nest, big as a hay-cock, in a withered tree, and a bevy of coots were flapping and gabbling in the weeds or between great leaves of the *Victoria Regia*—

an "escape" from the Durbar Gardens. Here were, as Mandeville hath it, "all manner of strange fowle"—divers and waders, after their kind, kingfishers and snaky-necked birds of the cormorant family, but no duck. They had seen the guns in the boat and were flying to and fro in companies across the lake, or settling, wise birds, in the glare of the sun on the water. The lake was swarming with them, but they seemed to know exactly how far a twelve-bore would carry. Perhaps their knowledge had been gained from the Englishman at the Residency. Later, as the sun left the lake and the hills began to glow like opals, the boat made her way to the shallow side of the lake, through fields of watergrass and dead lotus-raffle that rose as high as the bows, and clung lovingly about the rudder, and parted with the noise of silk when it is torn. There she waited for the fall of twilight when the duck would come home to bed, and the Englishman sprawled upon the cushions in deep content and laziness, as he looked across to where two marble Palaces floated upon the waters, and saw all the glory and beauty of the City, and wondered whether Tod, in cocked hat and stiff stock, had ever come shooting among the reeds, and, if so, how in the world he had ever managed to bowl over.

"Duck and drake, by Jove! Confiding beasts, weren't they? Hi! Lalla, jump out and get them!" It was a brutal thing, this double-barrelled murder perpetrated in the silence of the marsh when the kingly wild-duck came back from his wanderings with his mate at his side, but—but—the birds were very good to eat. After this and many other slaughters had been accomplished, the boat went back in the full dusk, down narrow water-lanes and across belts of weed, disturbing innumerable fowl on the road, till she reached open water and "the moon like a rick afire was rising over the dale," and—it was not the "whit, whit, whit" of the nightingale but the stately *"honk, honk"* of some wild geese, thanking their stars that these pestilent *shikaris* were going away.

If the Venetian owned the Pichola Sagar he might say with justice:—"See it and die." But it is better to live and go to dinner, and strike into a new life—that of the men who bear the hat-mark on their brow as plainly as the well-born native carries the *trisul* of Shiva.

They are of the same caste as the toilers on the Frontier—tough, bronzed men, with wrinkles at the corners of the eyes, gotten by looking across much sun-glare. When they would speak of horses they mention Arab ponies, and their talk, for the most part, drifts Bombaywards, or to Abu, which is their Simla. By these things the traveller may see that he is far away from the Presidency; and will presently learn that he is in a land where the railway is an incident and not an indispensable luxury. Folk tell strange stories of drives in bullock-carts in the rains, of break-downs in nullahs fifty miles from everywhere, and of elephants that used to sink "for rest and refreshment" half-way across swollen streams. Every place here seems fifty miles from everywhere, and the "legs of a horse" are regarded as the only natural means of locomotion. Also, and this to the Indian Cockney who is accustomed to the bleached or office man is curious, there are to be found many veritable "tiger men"—not story-spinners but such as have, in their wanderings from Bikaneer to Indore, dropped their tiger in the way of business. They are enthusiastic over princelings of little known fiefs, lords of austere estates perched on the tops of unthrifty hills, hard riders and good sportsmen. And five, six, yes fully nine hundred miles to the northward, lives the sister branch of the same caste—the men who swear by Pathan, Biluch and Brahui, with whom they have shot or broken bread.

There is a saying in Upper India that the

more desolate the country the greater the certainty of finding a Padre-Sahib. The proverb seems to hold good in Udaipur, where the Scotch Presbyterian Mission have a post, and others at Todgarh to the north and elsewhere. To arrive, under Providence, at the cure of souls through the curing of bodies certainly seems the most rational method of conversion; and this is exactly what the Missions are doing. Their Padre in Udaipur is also an M. D., and of him a rather striking tale is told. Conceiving that the City could bear another hospital in addition to the State one, he took furlough, went home, and there, by crusade and preaching, raised sufficient money for the scheme, so that none might say that he was beholden to the State. Returning, he built his hospital, a very model of neatness and comfort and, opening the operation-book, announced his readiness to see any one and every one who was sick. How the call was and is now responded to, the dry records of that book will show; and the name of the Padre-Sahib is honoured, as these ears have heard, throughout Udaipur and far around. The faith that sends a man into the wilderness, and the secular energy which enables him to cope with an evergrowing demand for medical aid, must, in time, find their reward. If patience and unwearying self-sacrifice carry any merit, they should do so soon. To-day the people are willing enough to be healed, and the general influence of the Padre-Sahib is very great. But beyond that. . . . Still it was impossible to judge aright.

VIII.

Divers Passages of Speech and Action whence the Nature, Arts and Disposition of the King and his Subjects may be observed.

IN this land men tell "sad stories of the death of Kings," not easily found elsewhere; and also speak of *sati*, which is generally supposed to be an "effete curiosity" as the Bengali said, in a manner which makes it seem very near and vivid. Be pleased to listen to some of the tales, but with all the names cut out, because a King has just as much right to have his family affairs respected as has a British householder paying income-tax.

Once upon a time, that is to say when the British power was well established in the land and there were railways, there was a King who lay dying for many days, and all, including the Englishmen about him, knew that his end was certain. But he had chosen to lie in an outer court or pleasure-house of his Palace; and with him were some twenty of his favourite wives. The place in which he lay was very near to the City; and there was a fear that his womenkind should, on his death, going mad with grief, cast off their veils and run out into the streets, uncovered before all men. In which case, nothing, not even the power of the Press, and the locomotive, and the telegraph, and cheap education and enlightened municipal councils, could have saved them from *sati,* for they were the wives of a King. So the Political did his best to induce the dying man to go to the Fort of the City, a safe place close to the regular zenana, where all the women could be kept within walls. He said that the air was better in the Fort, but the King refused; and that he would recover in the Fort; but the King refused. After some days, the latter turned and said:—"*Why* are you so keen, Sahib, upon getting my old bones up to the Fort?" Driven to his last defences, the Political said simply: — "Well, Maharana Sahib, the place is close to the road you see, and...." The King saw and said:—"Oh, *that's* it! I've been puzzling my brain for four days to find out what on earth you were driving at. I'll go to-night." "But there may be some difficulty," began the Political. "You think so," said the King. "If I only hold up my little finger, the women will obey me. Go now, and come back in five minutes, and all will be ready for departure." As a matter of fact, the Political withdrew for the space of fifteen minutes, and gave orders that the conveyances which he had kept in readiness day and night should be got ready. In fifteen minutes those twenty women, with their hand-maidens, were packed and ready for departure; and the King died later at the Fort, and nothing happened. Here the Englishman asked why a frantic woman must of necessity become *sati,* and felt properly abashed when he was told that she *must.* There was nothing else for her if she went out unveiled deliberately.

The rush-out forces the matter. And, indeed, if you consider the matter from a Rajput point of view, it does.

Then followed a very grim tale of the death of another King; of the long vigil by his bedside, before he was taken off the bed to die upon the ground; of the shutting of a certain mysterious door behind the bed-head, which shutting was followed by a rustle of women's dress; of a walk on the top of the Palace, to escape the heated air of the sick room; and then, in the grey dawn, the wail upon wail breaking from the zenana as the news of the King's death went in. "I never wish to hear anything more horrible and awful in my life. You could see nothing. You could only hear the poor wretches!" said the Political with a shiver.

The last resting-place of the Maharanas of Udaipur is at Ahar, a little village two miles east of the City. Here they go down in their robes of State, their horse following behind, and here the Political saw, after the death of a Maharana, the dancing-girls dancing before the poor white ashes, the musicians playing among the cenotaphs, and the golden hookah, sword and water-vessel laid out for the naked soul doomed to hover twelve days round the funeral pyre, before it could depart on its journey towards a fresh birth in the endless circle of the Wheel of Fate. Once, in a neighboring State it is said, one of the dancing-girls stole a march in the next world's precedence and her lord's affections, upon the legitimate queens. The affair happened, by the way, after the Mutiny, and was accomplished with great pomp in the light of day. Subsequently those who might have stopped it but did not, were severely punished. The girl said that she had no one to look to but the dead man, and followed him, to use Tod's formula, "through the flames." It would be curious to know what is done now and again among these lonely hills in the walled holds of the Thakurs.

But to return from the burning-ground to modern Udaipur, as at present worked under the Maharana and his Prime Minister Rae Punna Lal, *C. I. E.* To begin with, His Highness is a racial anomaly in that, judged by the strictest European standard, he is a man of temperate life, the husband of one wife whom he married before he was chosen to the throne after the death of the Maharana Sujjun Singh in 1884. Sujjun Singh died childless and gave no hint of his desires as to succession and—omitting all the genealogical and political reasons which would drive a man mad—Futteh Singh was chosen, by the Thakurs, from the Seorati Branch of the family which Sangram Singh II. founded. He is thus a younger son of a younger branch of a younger family, which lucid statement should suffice to explain everything. The man who could deliberately unravel the succession of any one of the Rajput States would be perfectly capable of clearing the politics of all the Frontier tribes from Jumrood to Quetta.

Roughly speaking, the Maharana and the Prime Minister—in whose family the office has been hereditary for many generations—divide the power of the State. They control, more or less, the Mahand Raj Sabha or Council of Direction and Revision. This is composed of many of the Rawats and Thakurs of the State, *and* the Poet Laureate who, under a less genial administration, would be presumably the Registrar. There are also District Officers, Officers of Customs, Superintendents of the Mint, Master of the Horses, and Supervisor of Doles, which last is pretty and touching. The State officers itself, and the Englishman's investigations failed to unearth any Bengalis. The Commandant of the State Army, about five thousand men of all arms, is a retired non-commissioned officer, a Mr. Lonergan; who, as the medals on his breast attest, has "done the State some service," and now in his old age rejoices in the rank of Major-General, and teaches the Maharaja's guns to make uncommonly good practice. The infantry are smart and well set up, while the Cavalry—rare thing in Native States—have a distinct notion of keeping their accoutrements clean. They are, further, well mounted on light wiry Mewar and Kathiawar horses. Incidentally, it may be mentioned that the Pathan comes down with his pickings from the Punjab to Udaipur, and finds a market there for animals that were much better employed in—but the complaint is a stale one. Let us see, later on, what the Jodhpur stables hold; and then formulate an indictment against the Government. So much for the indigenous administration of Udaipur. The one drawback in the present Maharaja, from the official point of view, is his want of education. He is a thoroughly good man, but was not brought up with a seat on the *guddee* before his eyes, consequently he is not an English-speaking man.

There is a story told of him, which is worth the repeating. An Englishman who flattered himself that he could speak the vernacular fairly well, paid him a visit and discoursed with a round mouth. The Maharana heard him politely, and turning to a satellite, demanded a translation; which was given. Then said the Maharana:—"Speak to him in *Angrezi*." The *Angrezi* spoken by the interpreter was the vernacular as the Sahibs speak it, and the Englishman, having ended his conference, departed abashed. But this backwardness is eminently suited to a place like Udaipur, and a "varnished" prince is not always a desirable thing. The curious and even startling simplicity of his life is worth preserving. Here is a specimen of one of his days. Rising at four—and the dawn can be bitterly chill—he bathes and prays after the custom of his race, and at six is ready to take in hand the first instalment of the day's work which comes before him through his Prime Minister, and occupies him for three or four hours till the first meal of the day is ready. At two o'clock he attends the Mahand Raj Sabha, and works till five, retiring at a healthily primitive hour. He is said to have his hand fairly firmly upon the reins of rule, and to know as much as most monarchs know of the way in which the revenues—about thirty lakhs—are disposed of. The Prime Minister's career has been a chequered and interesting one, including, *inter alia,* a dismissal from power (this was worked from behind the screen), and arrest and an attack with words which all but ended in his murder. He has not so much power as his predecessors had, for the reason that the present Maharaja allows little but tiger-shooting to distract him from the supervision of the State. His Highness, by the way, is a first-class shot, and has bagged eighteen tigers already. He preserves his game carefully, and permission to kill tigers is not readily obtainable.

A curious instance of the old order giving place to the new is in process of evolution and deserves notice. The Prime Minister's son, Futteh Lal, a boy of twenty years old, has been educated at the Mayo College, Ajmir, and speaks and writes English. There are few native officials in the State who do this; and the consequence is that the lad has won a very fair insight into State affairs, and knows generally what is going forward both in the Eastern and Western spheres of the little Court. In time he may qualify for direct administrative powers, and Udaipur will be added to the list of the States that are governed "English fash" as the irreverent Americans put it. What the end will be, after three generations of Princes and Dewans have been put through the mill of Rajkumar Colleges, those who live will learn.

More interesting is the question—For how long can the vitality of a people whose life was arms be suspended? Men in the North say that, by the favour of the Government, the Sikh Sirdars are rotting on their lands; and the Rajput Thakurs say of themselves that they are growing "rusty." The old, old problem forces itself on the most unreflective mind at every turn in the gay streets of Udaipur. A Frenchman might write:—"Behold there the horse of the Rajput—foaming, panting, caracoling, but always fettered with his head so majestic upon his bosom so amply filled with a generous heart. He rages, but he does not advance. See there the destiny of the Rajput who bestrides him, and upon whose left flank bounds the sabre useless—the haberdashery of the iron-monger only. Pity the horse in reason, for that life there is his *raison d'etre.* Pity ten thousand times more the Rajput, for he has no *raison d'etre.* He is an anachronism in a blue turban."

The Gaul might be wrong, but Tod wrote things which seem to support this view, in the days when he wished to make "buffer-states" of the land he loved so well.

Let us visit the Durbar Gardens, where little naked Cupids are trampling upon fountains of fatted fish, all in bronze, where there are cypresses and red paths, and a deer-park full of all varieties of deer, besides two growling, fluffy little panther cubs, a black panther who is the Prince of Darkness and a gentleman, and a terrace-full of tigers, bears, and Guzerat lions bought from the King of Oudh's sale.

On the best site in the Gardens is rising the Victoria Hall, the foundation-stone of which was laid by the Maharana on the 21st of June last. It is built after the designs of Mr. C. Thompson, Executive Engineer of the State, and will be in the Hindu-Saracenic style; having two fronts, west and north. In the former will be the principal entrance, approached by a flight of steps leading to a handsome porch of carved pillars supporting stone beams—the flat

Hindu arch. To the left of the entrance hall will be a domed octagonal tower eighty feet high, holding the principal staircase leading to the upper rooms. A corridor on the right of the entrance will lead to the museum, and immediately behind the entrance hall is the reading-room, 42 by 24 feet, and beyond it the library and office. To the right of the reading-room will be an open courtyard with a fountain in the centre, and, beyond the courtyard, the museum—a great hall, one hundred feet long. Over the library and the entrance hall will be private apartments for the Maharana, approached by a private staircase. The communication between the two upper rooms will be by a corridor running along the north front having a parapet of delicately cut pillars and cusped arches—the latter filled in with open tracery. Pity it is that the whole of this will have to be whitewashed to protect the stone from the weather. Over the entrance-porch, and projecting from the upper room, will be a very elaborately cut balcony supported on handsome brackets. Facing the main entrance will be a marble statue, nine feet high, of the Queen, on a white marble pedestal ten feet high. The statue is now being made at home by Mr. Birch, *R. A.* The cost of the whole will be about Rs. 80,000. Now, it is a curious thing that the statue of Her Majesty will be put some eighty feet below the level of the great bund that holds in the Pichola lake. But the bund is a firm one and has stood for many years.

Another public building deserves notice, and that is the Walter Hospital for native women, the foundation-stone of which was laid by the Countess of Dufferin on that memorable occasion when the Viceroy, behind Artillery Horses, covered the seventy miles from Chitor to Udaipur in under six hours. The building, by the same brain that designed the hall, will be ready for occupation in a month. It is in strict keeping with the canons of Hindu architecture externally, and has a high, well-ventilated waiting-room, out of which, to the right, are two wards for in-patients, and to the left a dispensary and consulting-room. Beyond these, again, is a third ward for in-patients. In a courtyard behind are a ward for low caste patients and the offices.

When all these buildings are completed, Udaipur will be dowered with three good hospitals, including the State's and the Padre's, and a first instalment of civilisation.

IX.

Of the Pig-drive which was a Panther-killing, and of the Departure to Chitor.

ABOVE the Durbar Gardens lie low hills, in which the Maharana keeps, very strictly guarded, his pig and his deer, and anything else that may find shelter in the low scrub or under the scattered boulders. These preserves are scientifically parcelled out with high red-stone walls; and, here and there, are dotted tiny shooting-boxes, in the first sense of the term—masonry sentry-boxes, in which five or six men may sit at ease and shoot. It had been arranged—to entertain the Englishmen who were gathered at the Residency to witness the investiture of the King with the G. C. S. I.—that there should be a little pig-drive in front of the Kala Odey or black shooting-box. The Rajput is a man and a brother, in respect that he will ride, shoot, eat pig and drink strong waters like an Englishman. Of the pig-hunting he makes almost a religious duty, and of the wine-drinking no less. Read how desperately they used to ride in Udaipur at the beginning of the century when Tod, always in his cocked hat be sure, counted up the tale of accidents at the end of the day's sport.

There is something unfair in shooting pig; but each man who went out consoled himself with the thought that it was utterly impossible to ride the brutes up the almost perpendicular hill-side, or down the rocky ravines, and that he individually would only go "just for the fun of the thing." Those who stayed behind made rude remarks on the subject of "pork butchers," and the dangers that attend shooting from a balcony. These were treated with the contempt they merited. There are ways and ways of slaying pig—from the orthodox method which begins with "*The Boar—The Boar—The mighty Boar!*" overnight, and ends with a shaky bridle hand next morn, to the sober and solitary pot-shot, at dawn, from a railway embankment running through river marsh; but the perfect way is this. Get a large four-horse break, and drive till you meet an unlimited quantity of pad-elephants waiting at the foot of rich hill-preserves. Mount slowly and with dignity, and go in swinging procession, by the marble-faced border of one of the most lovely lakes on earth. Strike off on a semi-road, semi-hill-torrent path through unthrifty thorny jungle, and so climb up and up and up, till you see, spread like a map below, the lake and the Palace and the City, hemmed in by the sea of hills that lies between Udaipur and Mount Abu a hundred miles away. Then take your seat in a comfortable chair, in a pukka, two-storeyed Grand Stand, with an awning spread atop to keep off the sun, while the Rawat of Amet and the Prime Minister's heir—no less—invite you to take your choice of the many rifles spread on a ledge at the front of the building. This, gentlemen who screw your pet ponies at early dawn after the sounder that vanishes into cover soon as sighted, or painfully follow the tiger through the burning heats of Mewar in May, this is shooting after the fashion of Ouida—in musk and ambergris and patchouli.

It is demoralising. One of the best and hardest riders of the Lahore Tent Club in the old days, as the boars of Bouli Lena Singh knew well, said openly:—"This is a first-class *bundobust,*" and fell to testing his triggers as though he had been a pot-hunter from his birth. Derision and threats of exposure moved him not. "Give me an arm-chair!" said he. "This is the proper way to deal with pig!" And he put up his feet on the ledge and stretched himself.

There were many weapons to have choice

among—from the double-barrelled .500 Express, whose bullet is a tearing, rending shell, to the Rawat of Amet's regulation military Martini-Henri. A profane public at the Residency had suggested clubs and saws as amply sufficient for the work in hand. Herein they were moved by envy, which passion was ten-fold increased when—but this comes later on. The beat was along a deep gorge in the hills, flanked on either crest by stone walls, manned with beaters. Immediately opposite the shooting-box, the wall on the upper or higher hill made a sharp turn downhill, contracting the space through which the pig would have to pass to a gut which was variously said to be from one hundred and fifty to four hundred yards across. Most of the shooting was up or downhill.

A philanthropic desire not to murder more Bhils than were absolutely necessary to maintain a healthy current of human life in the Hilly Tracts, coupled with a well-founded dread of the hinder, or horse, end of a double-barrelled .500 Express which would be sure to go off both barrels together, led the Englishman to take a gunless seat in the background; while a silence fell upon the party, and very far away up the gorge the heated afternoon air was cut by the shrill tremolo squeal of the Bhil beaters. Now a man may be in no sort or fashion a *shikari*—may hold Budhistic objections to the slaughter of living things—but there is something in the extraordinary noise of an agitated Bhil, which makes even the most peaceful of mortals get up and yearn, like Tartarin of Tarescon for "lions"—always at a safe distance be it understood. As the beat drew nearer, under the squealing—the "*ul-al-lu-lu-lu*"—was heard a long-drawn bittern-like boom of "*So-oor!*" "*So-oor!*" and the crashing of boulders. The guns rose in their places, forgetting that each and all had merely come "to see the fun," and began to fumble among the little mounds of cartridges under the chairs. Presently, tripping delicately among the rocks, a pig stepped out of a cactus-bush, and—the fusillade began. The dust flew and the branches chipped, but the pig went on—a blue-grey shadow almost undistinguishable against the rocks, and took no harm. "Sighting shots," said the guns sulkily; and the company mourned that the brute had got away. The beat came nearer, and then the listener discovered what the bubbling scream was like; for he forgot straightway about the beat and went back to the dusk of an Easter Monday in the gardens of the Crystal Palace, before the bombardment of Kars, "set piece ten thousand feet square," had been illuminated, and about five hundred 'Arries were tickling a thousand 'Arriets. Their giggling and nothing else was the noise of the Bhil. So curiously does Sydenham and Western Rajputana meet. Then came another pig, who was smitten to the death and rolled down among the bushes, drawing his last breath in a human and horrible manner.

But full on the crest of the hill, blown along—there is no other word to describe it—like a ball of thistle-down, passed a brown shadow, and men cried:—"*Bagheera!*" or "Panther!" according to their nationalities, and blazed. The shadow leaped the wall that had turned the pig downhill, and vanished among the cactus. "Never mind," said the Prime Minister's son consolingly, "we'll beat the other side of the hill afterwards and get him yet." "Oh! he's a mile off by this time," said the guns; but the Rawat of Amet, a magnificently handsome young man, smiled a sweet smile and said nothing. More pig passed and were slain, and many more broke back through the beaters who presently came through the cover in scores. They were in russet green and red uniform, each man bearing a long spear, and the hillside was turned on the instant to a camp of Robin Hood's foresters.

Then they brought up the dead from behind bushes and under rocks—among others a twenty-seven-inch brute who bore on his flank (all pigs shot in a beat are *ex-officio* boars) a hideous, half-healed scar, big as a man's hand, of a bullet wound. Express bullets are ghastly things in their effects, for, as the *shikari* is never tired of demonstrating, they knock the inside of animals into pulp.

The second beat, of the reverse side of the hill, had barely begun when the panther returnd—uneasily, as if something were keeping her back—much lower down the hill. Then the face of the Rawat of Amet changed, as he brought his gun up to his shoulder. Looking at him as he fired, one forgot all about the Mayo College at which he had been educated, and remembered only some trivial and out-of-date affairs, in which his forefathers had been concerned, when a bridegroom, with his bride at his side, charged down the slope of the Chitor road and died among Akbar's men. There are stories connected with the house of Amet, which are told in Mewar to-day. The young man's face, for as short a time as it takes to pull trigger and see where the bullet falls, was a light upon all these tales.

Then the mask shut down, as he clicked out

the cartridge and, very sweetly, gave it as his opinion that some other gun, and not his own, had bagged the panther, who lay shot through the spine, feebly trying to drag herself downhill into cover. It is an awful thing to see a big beast die, when the soul is wrenched out of the struggling body in ten seconds. Wild horses shall not make the Englishman disclose the exact number of shots that were fired. It is enough to say that four Englishmen, now scattered to the four winds of heaven, are each morally certain that he and he alone shot that panther. In time, when distance and the mirage of the sands of Jodhpur shall have softened the harsh outlines of truth, the Englishman who did *not* fire a shot will come to believe that he was the real slayer, and will carefully elaborate that lie.

A few minutes after the murder, a two-year old cub came trotting along the hill-side, and was bowled over by a very pretty shot behind the left ear and though the palate. Then the beaters' lances showed through the bushes, and the guns began to realise that they had allowed to escape, or had driven back by their fire, a multitude of pig.

This ended the beat, and the procession returned to the Residency to heap dead panthers upon those who had called them "pork butchers," and to stir up the lake of envy with the torpedo of brilliant description. The Englishman's attempt to compare the fusillade which greeted the panther to the continuous drumming of a ten-barrelled Nordenfeldt was, however, coldly received. So harshly is truth treated all the world over.

And then, after a little time, came the end, and a return to the road in search of new countries. But shortly before the departure, the Padre-Sahib, who knows every one in Udaipur, read a sermon in a sentence. The Maharana's investiture, which has already been described in the Indian papers, had taken place, and the carriages, duly escorted by the Erinpura Horse, were returning to the Residency. In a niche of waste land, under the shadow of the main gate, a place strewn with rubbish and shards of pottery, a dilapidated old man was trying to control his horse and a *hookah* on the saddle-bow. The blundering garron had been made restive by the rush past, and the *hookah* all but fell from the hampered hands. "See that man!" said the Padre tersely. "That's —— Singh. He intrigued for the throne not so very long ago." It was a pitiful little picture, and needed no further comment.

For the benefit of the loafer it should be noted that Udaipur will never be pleasant or accessible until the present Mail Contractors have been hanged. They are extortionate and untruthful, and their one set of harness and one tonga are as rotten as pears. However, the weariness of the flesh must be great indeed to make the wanderer blind to the beauties of a journey by clear starlight and in biting cold to Chitor. About six miles from Udaipur, the granite hills close in upon the road, and the air grows warmer until, with a rush and a rattle, the tonga swings through the great Dobarra, the gate in the double circle of hills round Udaipur on to the pastures of Mewar. More than once the Girwa has been a death-trap to those who rashly entered it; and an army has been cut up on the borders of the Pichola lake. Even now the genius of the place is strong upon the hills, and as he felt the cold air from the open ground without the barrier, the Englishman found himself repeating the words of one of the Hat-marked Tribe whose destiny kept him within the Dobarra. "You must have a *shouk* of some kind in these parts or you'll die." Very lovely is Udaipur, and thrice pleasant are a few days spent within her gates, but....read what Tod said who stayed two years behind the

Dobarra, and accepted the deserts of Marwar as a delightful change.

It is good to be free, a wanderer upon the highways, knowing not what to-morrow will bring forth—whether the walled-in niceties of an English household, rich in all that makes life fair and desirable, or a sleepless night in the society of a goods-*cum*-booking-office-*cum*-parcels-clerk, on fifteen rupees a month, who tells in stilted English the story of his official life, while the telegraph gibbers like a maniac once in an hour and then is dumb, and the pariah dogs fight and howl over the cotton-bales on the platform.

Verily, there is no life like life on the road—when the skies are cool and all men are kind.

X.

A little of the History of Chitor, and the Malpractices of a She-elephant.

THERE is a certain want of taste, an almost actual indecency, in seeing the sun rise on the earth. Until the heat-haze begins and the distances thicken, Nature is so very naked that the Actæon who has surprised her dressing, blushes. Sunrise on the plains of Mewar is an especially brutal affair.

The moon was burnt out and the air was bitterly cold, when the Englishman headed due east in his tonga, and the patient sowar behind nodded and yawned in the saddle. There was no warning of the day's advent. The horses were unharnessed, at one halting-stage, in the thick, soft shadows of night, and ere their successors had limped under the bar, a raw and cruel light was upon all things so that the Englishman could see every rent seam in the rocks around—see "even to the uttermost farthing." A little further, and he came upon the black bulk of Chitor between him and the morning sun. It has already been said that the Fort resembles a man-of-war. Every distant view heightens this impression, for the swell of the sides follows the form of a ship, and the bastions on the south wall make the sponsions in which the machine-guns are mounted. From bow to stern, the thing more than three miles long, is between three and five hundred feet high, and from one-half to one-quarter of a mile broad. Have patience, now, to listen to a rough history of Chitor.

In the beginning, no one knows clearly who scarped the hill-sides of the hill rising out of the bare plain, and made of it a place of strength. It is written that, eleven and a half centuries ago, Bappa Rawul, the demi-god whose stature was twenty cubits, whose loin-cloth was five hundred feet long, and whose spear was beyond the power of mortal man to lift, took Chitor from "Man Singh, the Mori Prince," and wrote the first chapter of the history of Mewar, which he received ready-made from Man Singh who, if the chronicles speak sooth, was his uncle. Many and very marvellous legends cluster round the name of Bappa Rawul; and he is said to have ended his days, far away from India, in Khorasan, where he married an unlimited number of the Daughters of Heth, and was the father of all the Nowshera

Pathans. Some who have wandered, by the sign-posts of inscription, into the fogs of old time, aver that, two centuries before Bappa Rawul took Chitor, the Mori Division of the Pramar Rajputs, who are the ruling family of Mewar, had found a hold in Bhilwar, and for four centuries before that time had ruled in Kathiawar; and had royally sacked and slain, and been sacked and slain in turn. But these things are for the curious and the scholar, and not for the reader who reads lightly. Nine princes succeeded Bappa, between 728 and 1068 *A. D.*, and among these was one Alluji, who built a Jain tower upon the brow of the hill, for in those days, though the Sun was worshipped, men were Jains.

And here they lived and sallied into the plains, and fought and increased the borders of their kingdom, or were suddenly and stealthily murdered, or stood shoulder to shoulder against the incursions of the "Devil men" from the north. In 1150 *A. D.* was born Samar Singh, and he married into the family of Prithi Raj, the last Hindu Emperor of Delhi, who was at feud, in regard to a succession question, with the Prince of Kanauj. In the war that followed, Kanauj, being hard pressed by Prithi Raj and Samar Singh, called Shahabuddin Ghori to his aid. At first, Samar Singh and Prithi Raj broke the army of the Northmen somewhere in the Lower Punjab, but two years later Shahabuddin came again, and, after three days' fighting on the banks of the Kaggar, slew Samar Singh, captured and murdered Prithi Raj, and sacked Delhi and Amber while Samar Singh's favorite queen became *sati* at Chitor. But another wife, a princess of Patun, kept her life, and when Shahabuddin sent down Kutbuddin to waste her lands, led the Rajput army, in person, from Chitor, and defeated Kutbuddin.

Then followed confusion, through eleven turbulent reigns, that the annalist has failed to unravel. Once in the years between 1193 and the opening of the fourteenth century, Chitor must have been taken by the Mussalman, for it is written that one prince "recovered Chitor and made the name of Rana to be recognized by all." Six princes were slain in battles against the Mussalman, in vain attempts to clear far away Gya from the presence of the infidel.

Then Ala-ud-din Khilji, the Pathan Emperor, swept the country to the Dekkan. In those days, and these things are confusedly set down as having happened at the end of the thirteenth century, a relative of Rana Lakhsman Singh, the then Rana of Chitor, had married a Rajput princess of Ceylon—Pudmini, "And she was fairest of all flesh on earth." Her fame was sung through the land by the poets, and she became, in some sort, the Helen of Chitor. Ala-ud-din heard of her beauty and promptly besieged the Fort. When he found his enterprise too difficult, he prayed that he might be permitted to see Pudmini's face in a mirror, and this wish, so says the tale, was granted. Knowing that the Rajput was a gentleman he entered Chitor almost unarmed, saw the face in the mirror, and was well treated; the husband of the fair Pudmini accompanying him, in return, to the camp at the foot of the hill. Like Raja Runjeet in the ballad the Rajput—

> "...... trusted a Mussalman's word
> Wah! Wah! Trust a liar to lie!
> Out of his eyrie they tempted my bird,
> Fettered his wings that he could not fly."

Pudmini's husband was caught, and Ala-ud-din demanded Pudmini as the price of his return. The Rajputs here showed that they too could scheme, and sent, in great state, Pudmini's litter to the besiegers' entrenchments. But there was no Pudmini in the litter, and the following of handmaidens was a band of seven hundred armed men. Thus, in the confusion of a camp-fight, Pudmini's husband was rescued, and Ala-ud-din's soldiery followed hard on his heels to the gates of Chitor, where the best and bravest on the rock were killed before Ala-ud-din withdrew, only to return soon after and, with a doubled army, besiege in earnest. His first attack men called the half-sack of Chitor, for, though he failed to win within the walls, he killed the flower of the Rajputs. The second attack ended in the first sack and the awful *sati* of the women on the rock.

When everything was hopeless and the very terrible Goddess, who lives in the bowels of Chitor, had spoken and claimed for death eleven out of the twelve of the Rana's sons, all who were young or fair women betook themselves to a great underground chamber, and the fires were lit and the entrance was walled up and they died. The Rajputs opened the gates and fought till they could fight no more, and Ala-ud-din the victorious entered a wasted and desolated city. He wrecked everything excepting only the palace of Pudmini and the old Jain tower before mentioned. That was all he could do, for there were few men alive of the defenders of Chitor when the day was won, and the women were ashes in the underground palace.

Ajai Singh, the one surviving son of Lakhsman Singh, had, at his father's insistence, escaped from Chitor to "carry on the line" when better days should come. He brought up Hamir, son of one of his elder brothers, to be a thorn in the side of the invader, and Hamir overthrew Maldeo, chief of Jhalore and vassal of Ala-ud-din, into whose hands Ala-ud-din had, not too generously, given what was left of Chitor. So the Sesodias came to their own again, and the successors of Hamir extended their kingdoms and rebuilt Chitor, as kings know how to rebuild cities in a land where human labour and life are cheaper than bread and water. For two centuries, saith Tod, Mewar flourished exceedingly and was the paramount kingdom of all Rajasthan. Greatest of all the successors of Hamir, was Kumbha Rana who, when the Ghilzai dynasty was rotting away and Viceroys declared themselves kings, met, defeated, took captive, and released without ransom, Mahmoud of Malwa. Kumbha Rana built a Tower of Victory, nine stories high, to commemorate this and the other successes of his reign, and the tower stands to-day a mark for miles across the plains. Of this, more hereafter.

But the well-established kingdom weakened, and the rulers took favourites and disgusted their best supporters—after the immemorial custom of too prosperous rulers. Also they murdered one another. In 1535 *A. D.* Bahadur Shah, King of Gujarat, seeing the decay, and remembering how one of his predecessors, together with Mahmoud of Malwa, had been humbled by Mewar in years gone by, set out to take his revenge of Time and Mewar then ruled by Rana Bikrmajit, who had made a new capital at Deola. Bikrmajit did not stay to give battle in that place. His chiefs were out of hand, and Chitor was the heart and brain of Mewar; so he marched thither, and the Gods were against him. Bahadur Shah mined one of the Chitor bastions and wiped out in the explosion the Hara Prince of Boondee with five hundred followers. Jowahir Bae, Bikrmajit's mother headed a sally from the walls and was slain. There were Frank gunners among Bahadur Shah's forces, and they hastened the end. The Rajputs made a second *johur* greater than the *johur* of Pudmini; and thirteen thousand were blown up in the magazines, or stabbed or poisoned, before the gates were opened and the defenders rushed down.

Out of the carnage was saved Udai Singh, a babe of the Blood Royal, who grew up to be a coward and a shame to his line. The story of his preservation is written large in Tod, and Edwin Arnold sings it. Read it, who are interested. But, when Udai Singh came to the throne of Chitor, through blood and mis-rule, after Bahadur Shah had withdrawn from the wreck of the Fort, Akbar sat on the throne of Delhi, and it was written that few people should withstand the "Guardian of Mankind." Moreover, Udai Singh was the slave of a woman. It was Akbar's destiny to subdue the Rajputs and to win many of them to his own service; sending a Rajput Prince of Amber to get him Arrakan. Akbar marched against Chitor once and was repulsed; the woman who ruled Udai Singh heading a charge against the besiegers because of the love she bore to her lover. Something of this sort had happened in Ala-ud-din's time, and, like Ala-ud-din, Akbar returned and sat down, in a huge camp, before Chitor in 1568 *A. D.* Udai Singh fled what was coming; and because the Goddess of Chitor demands always that a crowned head must fall if the defence of her home is to be successful, Chitor fell as it had fallen before—in a *johur* of thousands, a last rush of the men, and the entry of the conqueror into a reeking, ruined slaughter-pen. Akbar's sack was the most terrible of the three, for he killed everything that had life upon the rock, and wrecked and overturned and spoiled. The wonder, the lasting wonder, is that he did not destroy Kumbha Rana's Tower of Victory and memorial of the defeat of a Mahomedan prince. With the third sack the glory of Chitor departed, and Udai Singh founded himself a new capital, the city of Udaipur Though Chitor was recovered in Jehangir's time by Udai Singh's grandson, it was never again made the capital of Mewar. It stood and rooted where it stood, till enlightened and loyal feudatories in the present years of grace, made attempts, with the help of Executive Engineers, to sweep it up and keep it in repair. The above is roughly, very roughly indeed, the tale of the sacks of Chitor.

Follows an interlude, for the study even of inaccurate history is indigestible to many. There was an elephant at Chitor, to take birds of passage up the hill, and she—she was fifty-one years old and her name was Gerowlia—came to the dak-bungalow for the Englishman. Let not the word dak-bungalow deceive any man into believing that there is even moderate comfort at Chitor. Gerowlia waited in the sunshine, and chuckled to herself like a female pauper when she receives snuff. The *mahout* said that he would go away for a drink of water. So he walked, and walked, and walked, till he disappeared on the stone-strewn plains, and the Englishman was left alone with Gerowlia aged fifty-one. She had been tied by the chain on her near hind-leg to a pillar of the verandah; but the string was *moonj* string only, and more an emblem of authority than a means of restraint. When she had thoroughly exhausted all the resources of the country within range of her trunk, she ate up the string and began to investigate the verandah. There was more *moonj* string, and she ate it all, while the *mistri* who was repairing the dak-bungalow cursed her and her ancestry from afar. About this time the Englishman was roused to a knowledge of the business, for Gerowlia, having exhausted the string, tried to come into the verandah. She had, most unwisely, been pampered with biscuits an hour before. The *mistri* stood on an outcrop of rock and said angrily:—"See what damage your *hathi* has done, Sahib!" "'Tisn't my *hathi*," said the Sahib plaintively. "You ordered it," quoth the *mistri*, "and it has been here ever so long, eating up everything." Herewith he threw pieces of stone at Gerowlia and went away. It is a terrible thing to be left alone with an unshackled elephant, even though she be a venerable spinster. Gerowlia moved round the dak-bungalow, blowing her nose in a nervous and undecided manner and, presently, found some more string, which she ate. This was too much. The Englishman went out and spoke to her. She opened her mouth and salaamed; meaning thereby "biscuits." So long as she remained in this position she could do no harm.

Imagine a boundless rock-strewn plain, broken here and there by low hills, dominated by the rock of Chitor and bisected by a single, metre-gauge railway track running into the Infinite, and unrelieved by even a way-inspector's trolly. In the fore-ground put a brand-new dak-bungalow furnished with a French bedstead and nothing else; and, in the verandah, place an embarrassed Englishman, smiling into the open mouth of an idiotic female elephant. But Gerowlia could not live on smiles alone. Finding that no food was forthcoming, she shut her mouth and renewed her attempts to get into the verandah and ate more *moonj* string. To say "H!" to an elephant is a misdirected courtesy. It quickens the pace, and, if you flick her on the trunk with a wet towel, she curls the trunk out of harm's way. Special education is necessary. A little breechless boy passed, carrying a lump of stone. "Hit on the feet, Sahib!" said he; "Hit on the feet!" Gerowlia had by this time nearly scraped off her pad and there were no signs of the *mahout.* The Englishman went out and found a tent-peg, and returning, in the extremity of his wrath, smote her bitterly on the nails of the near forefoot.

Then, as Rider Haggard used to say—though the expression was patented by at least one writer before he made it his own—a curious thing happened. Gerowlia held up her foot to be beaten, and made the most absurd noises—squawked, in fact, exactly like an old lady who has narrowly escaped being run over. She backed out of the verandah, still squawking, on three feet and in the open held up near and off forefoot alternately to be beaten. It was very pitiful, for one swing of her trunk could have knocked the Englishman flat. He ceased whacking her, but she squawked for some minutes and then fell placidly asleep in the sunshine. When the *mahout* returned, he beat her for breaking her tether exactly as the Englishman had done, but much more severely, and the ridiculous old thing hopped on three legs for fully five minutes. "Come along, Sahib!" said the *mahout,* "I will show this mother of bastards who is the *mahout.* Fat daughter of the Devil, sit down! You would eat string, would you? How does the iron taste?" And he gave Gerowlia a headache, which affected her temper all through the afternoon. She set off, across the railway line which runs below the rock of Chitor, into broken ground cut up with *nullahs* and covered with low scrub, over which it would have been difficult to have taken a sure-footed horse—so fragmentary and disconnected was its nature.

XI.

Proves conclusively the Existence of the Dark Tower visited by Childe Rolande, and of "Bogey" who frightens Children.

THE Gamberi river—clear as a trout stream—runs through the waste round Chitor, and is spanned by an old bridge, very solid and massive, said to have been built before the sack of Ala-ud-din. The bridge is in the middle of the stream—the floods have raced round either end of it—and is reached by a steeply sloping stone causeway. From the bridge to the new town of Chitor, which lies at the foot of the hill, runs a straight and well-kept road, flanked on either side by the scattered remnants of old houses, and, here and there, fallen temples. The road, like the bridge, is no new thing, and is wide enough for twenty horsemen to ride abreast.

New Chitor is a very dirty, and apparently thriving, little town, full of grain-merchants and sellers of arms. The ways are barely wide enough for the elephant of dignity and the little brown babies of impudence. The Englishman went through, always on a slope painfully accentuated by Gerowlia who, with all possible respect to her years, must have been a baggage-animal and no true Sahib's mount. Let the local Baedeker speak for a moment:—"The ascent to Chitor, which begins from within the south-east angle of the town, is nearly a mile to the upper gate, with a slope of about 1 in 15. There are two zig-zag bends, and on the three portions thus formed, are seven gates, of which one, however, has only the basement left." This is the language of fact which, very properly, leaves out of all account the Genius of the Place who sits at the gate nearest the new city and is with the sightseer throughout. The first impression of repulsion and awe is given by a fragment of tumbled sculpture close to a red daubed *lingam,* near the Padal Pol or lowest gate. It is a piece of frieze, and the figures of the men are worn nearly smooth by time. What is visible is finely and frankly obscene to an English mind.

The road is protected on the *khud* side by a thick stone wall, loopholed for musketry, one aperture to every two feet, between fifteen and twenty feet high. This wall is being repaired throughout its length by the Maharana of Udaipur. On the hill side, among the boulders, loose stones and *dhao*-scrub, lies stone wreckage that must have come down from the brown bastions above.

As Gerowlia laboured up the stone-shod slope, the Englishman wondered how much life had flowed down this sluice of battles, and been lost at the Padal Pol—the last and lowest gate—where, in the old days, the besieging armies put their best and bravest battalions. Once at the head of the lower slope, there is a clear run-down of a thousand yards with no chance of turning aside either to the right or left. Even as he wondered, he was brought abreast of two stone chhatris, each carrying a red daubed stone. They were the graves of two very brave men, Jeemal of Bednore, and Kalla, who fell in Akbar's sack fighting like Rajputs. Read the story of their deaths, and learn what manner of warriors they were. Their graves were all that spoke openly of the hundreds of struggles on the lower slope where the fight was always fiercest.

At last, after half an hour's climb, the main gate, the Ram Pol, was gained, and the Englishman passed into the City of Chitor and—then and there formed a resolution, since broken, not to write one word about it for fear that he should be set down as a babbling and a gushing enthusiast. Objects of archæological interest are duly described in an admirable little book of Chitor which, after one look, the Englishman abandoned. One cannot "do" Chitor with a guide-book. The Padre of the English Mission to Jehangir said the best that was to be said, when he described the place three hundred years ago, writing quaintly:—"Chitor, an ancient great kingdom, the chief city so called which standeth on a mighty high hill, flat on the top, walled about at the least ten English miles. There appear to this day above a hundred ruined churches and divers fair palaces which are lodged in like manner among their ruins, as many Englishmen by the observation have guessed. Its chief inhabitants to-day are Zum and Ohim, birds and wild beasts, but the stately ruins thereof give a shadow of its beauty while it flourished in its pride." Gerowlia struck into a narrow pathway, forcing herself through garden-trees and disturbing the peacocks. An evil guide-man on the ground waved his hand, and began to speak; but was silenced. The death of Amber was as nothing to the death of Chitor—a body whence the life had been driven by riot and sword. Men had parcelled the gardens of her palaces and the courtyards of her temples into fields; and cattle grazed among the remnants of the shattered tombs. But over all—over rent bastion, split temple-wall, pierced roof and prone pillar—lay the "shadow of its beauty while it flourished in its pride." The Englishman walked into a stately palace of many rooms, where the sunlight streamed in through wall and roof, and up crazy stone stairways, held together, it seemed, by the marauding trees. In one bastion, a wind-sown peepul had wrenched a thick slab clear of the wall, but held it tight pressed in a crook of a branch, as a man holds down a fallen enemy under his elbow, shoulder and forearm. In another place, a strange, uncanny wind, sprung from nowhere, was singing all alone among the pillars of what may have been a Hall of Audience. The Englishman wandered so far in one palace that he came to an almost black-dark room, high up in a wall, and said proudly to himself:—"I must be the first man who has been here;" meaning thereby no harm or insult to any one. But he tripped and fell, and as he put out his hands, he felt that the stairs had been worn hollow and smooth by the tread of innumerable naked feet. Then he was afraid, and came away very quickly, stepping delicately over fallen friezes and bits of sculptured men, so as not to offend the dead; and was mightily relieved when he recovered his elephant and allowed the guide to take him to Kumbha Rana's Tower of Victory.

This stands, like all things in Chitor, among ruins, but time and the other enemies have been good to it. It is a Jain edifice, nine storeys high, crowned atop—Was this designed insult or undesigned repair?—with a purely Mahomedan dome, wherein the pigeons and the bats live. Excepting this blemish, the Tower of Victory is nearly as fair as when it left the hands of the builder whose name has not been handed down to us. It is to be observed here that the first, or more ruined, Tower of Victory, built in Alluji's days, when Chitor was comparatively young, was raised by some pious Jain, as proof of conquest over things spiritual. The second tower is more worldly in intent.

Those who care to look, may find elsewhere a definition of its architecture and its more striking peculiarities. It was in kind, but not in degree, like the Jugdesh Temple at Udaipur, and, as it exceeded it in magnificence, so its effect upon the mind was more intense. The confusing intricacy of the figures with which it was wreathed from top to bottom, the recurrence of the one calm face, the God enthroned, holding the Wheel of the Law, and the appalling lavishness of decoration, all worked towards the instilment of fear and aversion.

Surely this must have been one of the objects of the architect. The tower, in the arrangement of its stairways, is like the interior of a Chinese carved ivory puzzle-ball. The idea given is that, even while you are ascending, you are wrapping yourself deeper and deeper in the tangle of a mighty maze. Add to this the half-light, the thronging armies of sculptured figures, the mad profusion of design splashed as impartially upon the undersides of the stone window-slabs as upon the door-beam of the threshold—add, most abhorrent of all, the slippery sliminess of the walls worn smooth by naked men, and you will understand that the tower is not a soothing place to visit. The Englishman fancied presumptuously that he had, in a way, grasped the builder's idea; and when he came to the top storey and sat among the pigeons his theory was this:—To attain power, wrote the builder of old, in sentences of fine stone, it is necessary to pass through all sorts of close-packed horrors, treacheries, battles and insults, in darkness and without knowledge whether the road leads upward or into a hopeless *cul-de-sac*. Kumbha Rana must many times have climbed to the top storey, and looked out towards the uplands of

Malwa on the one side and his own great Mewar on the other, in the days when all the rock hummed with life and the clatter of hooves upon the stony ways, and Mahmoud of Malwa was safe in hold. How he must have swelled with pride—fine insolent pride of life and rule and power,—power not only to break things but to compel such builders as those who piled the tower to his royal will! There was no decoration in the top storey to bewilder or amaze—nothing but well-grooved stone-slabs, and a boundless view fit for kings who traced their ancestry—

> "From times when forth from the sunlight, the first of our kings came down,
> And had the earth for his footstool, and wore the stars for his crown."

The builder had left no mark behind him—not even a mark on the threshold of the door, or a sign in the head of the topmost step. The Englishman looked in both places, believing that those were the places generally chosen for mark-cutting. So he sat and meditated on the beauties of kingship, and the unholiness of Hindu art, and what power a shadow-land of lewd monstrosities had upon those who believed in it, and what Lord Dufferin, who is the nearest approach to a king in this India, must have thought when

A.-D.-C.'s clanked after him up the narrow steps. But the day was wearing, and he came down—in both senses—and, in his descent, the carven things on every side of the tower and above and below, once more took hold of and perverted his fancy, so that he arrived at the bottom in a frame of mind eminently fitted for a descent into the Gau-Mukh, which is nothing more terrible than a little spring, falling into a reservoir, in the side of the hill.

He stumbled across more ruins and passed between tombs of dead Ranis, till he came to a flight of steps, built out and cut out from rock, going down as far as he could see into a growth of trees on a terrace below him. The stone of the steps had been worn and polished by naked feet till it showed its markings clearly as agate; and where the steps ended in a rock-slope, there was a visible glair, a great snail track, upon the rocks. It was hard to keep safe footing on the sliminess. The air was thick with the sick smell of stale incense, and grains of rice were scattered upon the steps. But there was no one to be seen. Now this in itself was not specially alarming; but the Genius of the Place must be responsible for making it so. The Englishman slipped and bumped on the rocks, and arrived, more suddenly than he desired, upon the edge of a dull blue tank, sunk between walls of timeless masonry. In a slabbed-in recess, water was pouring through a shapeless stone gargoyle, into a trough; which trough again dripped into the tank. Almost under the little trickle of water, was the loathsome Emblem of Creation, and there were flowers and rice around it. Water was trickling from a score of places in the cut face of the hill, oozing between the edges of the steps and welling up between the stone slabs of the terrace. Trees sprouted in the sides of the tank and hid its surroundings. It seemed as though the descent had led the Englishman, *firstly,* two thousand years away from his own century, and *secondly,* into a trap, and that he would fall off the polished stones into the stinking tank, or that the Gau-Mukh would continue to pour water placidly until the tank rose up and swamped him, or that some of the stone slabs would fall forward and crush him flat.

Then he was conscious of remembering, with peculiar and unnecessary distinctness, that, from the Gau-Mukh, a passage led to the subterranean chambers in which fair Pudmini and her handmaids had slain themselves. Also, that Tod had written and the Station-master at Chitor had said, that some sort of devil, or ghoul, or some thing, stood at the entrance of that approach. All of which was a nightmare bred in full day, and folly to boot; but it was the fault of the Genius of the Place, who made the Englishman feel that he had done a great wrong in trespassing into the very heart and soul of all Chitor. And, behind him, the Gau-Mukh guggled and choked like a man in his death-throe. The Englishman endured as long as he could—about two minutes. Then it came upon him that he must go quickly out of this place of years and blood—must get back to the afternoon sunshine, and Gerowlia, and the dak-bungalow with the French bedstead. He desired no archæological information, he wished to take no notes, and, above all, he did not care to look behind him, where stood the reminder that he was no better than the beasts that perish. But he had to cross the smooth, worn rocks, and he felt their sliminess through his boot-soles. It was as though he were treading on the soft, oiled skin of a Hindu. As soon as the steps gave refuge, he floundered up them, and so came out of the Gau-Mukh, bedewed with that perspiration which follows alike on honest toil or—childish fear.

"This," said he to himself, "is absurd!" and sat down on the fallen top of a temple to review the situation. But the Gau-Mukh had disappeared. He could see the dip in the ground, and the beginning of the steps, but nothing more.

In defence, it may be urged that there is moral, just as much as there is mine, choke-damp. If you get into a place laden with the latter you die, and if into the home of the former you......behave unwisely, as constitution and temperament prompt. If any man doubt this, let him sit for two hours in a hot sun on an elephant, stay half-an-hour in the Tower of Victory, and then go down into the Gau-Mukh, which, it must never be forgotten, is merely a set of springs "three or four in number, issuing from the cliff face at cow-mouth carvings, now mutilated. The water evidently percolating from the Hathi Kund above, falls first in an old pillared hall and thence into the masonry reservoir below, eventually, when abundant enough, supplying a little waterfall lower down." That, Gentlemen and Ladies, on the honour of one who has been frightened of the dark in broad daylight, is the Gau-Mukh, as though photographed.

The Englishman regained Gerowlia and demanded to be taken away, but Gerowlia's driver went forward instead and showed him a new Mahal just built by the present Maharana. If a fourth sack of Chitor could be managed for a Viceroy's edification, the blowing up of the new Mahal would supply a pleasant evening's entertainment. Near the Mahal lie the remains of the great tanks of Chitor, for the hill has, through a great part of its length, a depression in the centre which, by means of bunds, stored, in the old time, a full supply of water. A general keeping in order is visible throughout many of the ruins; and, in places, a carriage-drive is being constructed. Carriage-drives, however, do not consort well with Chitor and the "shadow of her ancient beauty." The return journey, past temple after temple and palace upon palace, began in the failing light, and Gerowlia was still blundering up and down narrow bye-paths—for she possessed all an old woman's delusion as to the slimness of her waist—when the twilight fell, and the smoke from the town below began to creep up the brown flanks of Chitor, and the jackals howled. Then the sense of desolation, which had been strong enough in all conscience in the sunshine, began to grow and grow:—

> "The sun's eye had a sickly glare,
> The earth with age was wan,
> The skeletons of ages stood
> Around that lonely man."

Near the Ram Pol there was some semblance of a town with living people in it, and a priest sat in the middle of the road and howled aloud upon his Gods, until a little boy came and laughed in his face heretically, and he went away grumbling. This touch was deeply refreshing; in the contemplation of it, the Englishman clean forgot that he had overlooked the gathering in of materials for an elaborate statistical, historical, geographical account of Chitor. All that remained to him was a shuddering reminiscence of the Gau-Mukh and two lines of the "Holy Grail."

> "And up into the sounding halls he passed,
> But nothing in the sounding halls he saw."

Post Scriptum.—There was something very uncanny about the Genius of the Place. He dragged an ease-loving egotist out of the French bedstead with the gilt knobs at head and foot, into a more than usually big folly—nothing less than a seeing of Chitor by moonlight. There was no possibility of getting Gerowlia out of *her* bed, and a mistrust of the Maharana's soldiery who in the day time guarded the gates, prompted the Englishman to avoid the public way, and scramble straight up the hillside, along an attempt at a path which he had noted from Gerowlia's back. There was no one to interfere, and nothing but an infinity of pestilent nullahs and loose stones to check. Owls came out and hooted at him, and animals ran about in the dark and made uncouth noises. It was an idiotic journey, and it ended—Oh horror! in that unspeakable Gau-Mukh—this time entered from the opposite or brushwooded side, as far as could be made out in the dusk and from the chuckle of the water which, by night, was peculiarly malevolent.

Escaping from this place, crab-fashion, the Englishman crawled into Chitor and sat upon a flat tomb till the moon, a very inferior and second-hand one, rose, and turned the city of the dead into a city of scurrying ghouls—in sobriety, jackals. Also, the ruins took strange shapes and shifted in the half light and cast objectionable shadows.

It was easy enough to fill the rock with the people of old times, and a very beautiful account of Chitor restored, made out by the help of Tod, and bristling with the names of the illustrious dead, would undoubtedly have been written, had not a woman, a living, breathing woman, stolen out of a temple—What was she doing in that galley?—and screamed in piercing and public-spirited fashion. The Englishman got off the tomb and departed rather more noisily than a jackal; feeling for the moment that he was not much better. Somebody opened a door with a crash, and a man cried out:—"Who is there?" But the cause of the disturbance was, for his sins, being most horribly scratched by some thorny scrub over the edge of the hill—there are no bastions worth speaking of near the Gau-Mukh—and the rest was partly rolling, partly scrambling, and mainly bad language.

When you are too lucky sacrifice something, a beloved pipe for choice, to Ganesh. The Englishman has seen Chitor by moonlight—not the best moonlight truly, but the watery glare of a nearly spent moon—and his sacrifice to Luck is this. He will never try to describe what he has seen—but will keep it as a love-letter, a thing for one pair of eyes only—a memory that few men to-day can be sharers in. And does he, through this fiction, evade insulting, by the dauberie of pen and ink, a scene as lovely, wild, and unmatchable as any that mortal eyes have been privileged to rest upon?

An intelligent and discriminating public are perfectly at liberty to form their own opinions.

XII.

Contains the History of the Bhumia of Jharwasa, and the Record of a Visit to the House of Strange Stories. Demonstrates the Felicity of Loaferdom, which is the veritable Companionship of the Indian Empire, and proposes a Scheme for the better Officering of two Departments.

COME away from the monstrous gloom of Chitor and escape northwards. The place is unclean and terrifying. Let us catch To-day by both hands and return to the Station-master—who is also booking-parcels and telegraph-clerk, and who never seems to go to bed—and to the comfortably wadded bunks of the Rajputana-Malwa line.

While the train is running, be pleased to listen to the perfectly true story of the *bhumia* of Jharwasa, which is a story the sequel whereof has yet to be written. Once upon a time, a Rajput landholder, a *bhumia,* and a Mahomedan *jaghirdar,* were next-door neighbours in Ajmir territory. They hated each other thoroughly for many reasons, all connected with land; and the *jaghirdar* was the bigger man of the two. In those days, it was the law that victims of robbery or dacoity should be reimbursed by the owner of the lands on which the affair had taken place. The ordinance is now swept away as impracticable. There was a highway robbery on the *bhumia's* holding; and he vowed that it had been "put up" by the Mahomedan who, he said, was an Ahab. The reive-gelt payable nearly ruined the Rajput, and he, labouring under a galling grievance or a groundless suspicion, fired the *jaghirdar's* crops, was detected and brought up before the English Judge who gave him four years' imprisonment. To the sentence was appended a recommendation that, on release, the Rajput should be put on heavy securities for good behaviour. "Otherwise," wrote the Judge, who seems to have known the people he was dealing with, "he will certainly kill the *jaghirdar.*" Four years passed, and the *jaghirdar* obtained wealth and consideration, and was made, let us say, a Khan Bahadur, and an Honorary Magistrate; but the *bhumia* remained in gaol and thought over the highway robbery. When the day of release came, a new Judge hunted up his predecessor's finding and recommendation, and would have put the *bhumia* on security. "Sahib," said the *bhumia,* "I have no people. I have been in gaol. What am I now? And who will find security for me? If you will send me back to gaol again I can do nothing, and I have no friends." So they released him, and he went away into an outlying village and borrowed a sword from one house, and had it sharpened in another, for love. Two days later fell the birthday of the Khan Bahadur and the Honorary Magistrate, and his friends and servants and dependants made a little durbar and did him honour after the native custom. The *bhumia* also attended the levee, but no one knew him, and he was stopped at the door of the courtyard by the servant. "Say that the *bhumia* of Jharwasa has come to pay his salaams," said he. They let him in, and in the heart of Ajmir City, in broad daylight, and before all the *jaghirdar's* household, he smote off his enemy's head so that it rolled upon the ground. Then he fled, and though they raised the country-side against him he was never caught, and went into Bikanir.

Five years later, word came to Ajmir that Chimbo Singh, the *bhumia* of Jharwasa, had taken service under the Thakur Sahib of Palitana. The case was an old one, and the chances of identification musty, but the suspected was caught and brought in, and one of the leading native barristers of the Bombay Bar was retained to defend him. He said nothing and continued to say nothing, and the case fell through. He is believed to be "wanted" now for a fresh murder committed within the last few months, out Bikanir way.

And now that the train has reached Ajmir, the Crewe of Rajputana, whither shall a tramp turn his feet? The Englishman set his stick on end, and it fell with its point North-West as nearly as might be. This being translated, meant Jodhpur, which is the city of the Hounhnhyms and, that all may be in keeping, the occasional resting-place of fugitive Yahoos. If you would enjoy Jodhpur thoroughly, quit at Ajmir the decent conventionalities of "station" life, and make it your business to move among gentlemen—gentlemen in the Ordnance of the Commissariat, or, better still, gentlemen on the Railway. At Ajmir, gentlemen will tell you what manner of place Jodhpur is, and their accounts, though flavoured with crisp and curdling oaths, are amusing. In their eyes the desert that rings the city has no charms, and they discuss affairs of the State, as they understand them, in a manner that would curl the hair on a Political's august head. Jodhpur has been, but things are rather better now, a much-favoured camping ground for the light-cavalry of the road—the loafers with a certain amount of brain and great assurance. The explanation is simple. There are more than four hundred horses in His Highness's city stables alone; and where the Hounhnhym is, there also will be the Yahoo. This is sad but true.

Besides the Uhlans who come and go on Heaven knows what mysterious errands, there are bag-men travelling for the big English firms. Jodhpur is a good customer, and purchases all sorts of things, more or less useful, for the State or its friends. These are the gentlemen to know, if you would understand something of matters which are not written in reports.

The Englishman took a train from Ajmir to Marwar Junction, which is on the road to Mount Abu, westward from Ajmir, and at five in the morning, under pale moonlight, was uncarted at the beginning of the Jodhpur State Railway—one of the quaintest little lines that ever ran a locomotive. It is the Maharaja's very own, and pays about ten per cent.; but its quaintness does not lie in these things. It is worked with rude economy, and started life by singularly and completely falsifying the Government estimates for its construction. An intelligent Bureau asserted that it could not be laid down for less than—but the error shall be glossed over. It was laid down for a little more than seventeen thousand rupees a mile, with the help of second-hand rails and sleepers; and it is currently asserted that the Station-masters are flagmen, pointsmen, ticket-collectors and everything else, except platforms and lamp-rooms. As only two trains are run in the twenty-four hours, this economy of staff does not matter in the least. The State line, with the comparatively new branch to the Pachbadra salt-pits, pays handsomely, and is exactly suited to the needs of its users. True, there is a certain haziness as to the hour of starting, but this allows laggards more time, and fills the packed carriages to overflowing.

From Marwar Junction to Jodhpur, the train leaves the Aravalis and goes northwards into "the region of death" that lies beyond the Luni River. Sand, *ak* bushes, and sand-hills, varied with occasional patches of unthrifty cultivation, make up the scenery. Rain has been very scarce in Marwar this year, and the country, consequently, shows at its worst, for almost every square mile of the kingdom nearly as large as Scotland is dependent on the sky for its crops. In a good season, a large village can pay from seven to nine thousand rupees revenue without blenching. In a bad one, "all the king's horses and all the king's men" may think themselves lucky if they raise "rupees fifteen only" from the same place. The fluctuation is startling.

From a country-side, which to the uninitiated seems about as valuable as a stretch of West African beach, the State gets a revenue of nearly forty lakhs; and men who know the country vow that it has not been one tithe exploited, and that there is more to be made from salt and the marble and—curious thing in this wilderness—good forest conservancy, than an open-handed Durbar dreams of. An amiable weakness for unthinkingly giving away villages where ready cash failed, has somewhat hampered the revenue in past years; but now—and for this the Maharaja deserves great credit—Jodhpur has a large and genuine surplus, and a very compact little scheme of railway extension. Before turning to a consideration of the City of Jodhpur, hear a true story in connection with the Hyderabad-Pachbadra project which those interested in the scheme may lay to heart.

His State line, his "ownest own," as has been said, very much delighted the Maharaja who, in one or two points, is not unlike Sir

Theodore Hope of sainted memory. Pleased with the toy, he said effusively, in words which may or may not have reached the ears of the Hyderabad-Pachbadra people:—"This is a good business. If the Government will give me independent jurisdiction, I'll make and open the line straightaway from Pachbadra to the end of my dominions, *i. e.,* all but to Hyderabad."

Then "up and spake an elder knight, sat at the King's right knee," who knew something about the railway map of India, and the Controlling Power of strategical lines:—"Maharaja Sahib—here is the Indus Valley State and here is the Bombay-Baroda. Where would you be?" "By Jove," quoth the Maharaja, though he swore by quite another god: "I see!" and thus he abandoned the idea of a Hyderabad line, and turned his attention to an extension to Nagore, with a branch to the Makrana marble-quarries which are close to the Sambhar salt lake near Jeypore. And, in the fulness of time, that extension will be made and perhaps extended to Bahawalpur.

The Englishman came to Jodhpur at mid-day, in a hot, fierce sunshine that struck back from the sands and the ledges of red-rock, as though it were May instead of December. The line scorned such a thing as a regular ordained terminus. The single track gradually melted away into the sands. Close to the station was a grim stone dak-bungalow, and in the verandah stood a brisk, bag-and-flask-begirdled individual, cracking his joints with excess of irritation. He was also snorting like an impatient horse.

Nota Bene.—When one is on the road it is above all things necessary to "pass the time o'day" to fellow-wanderers. Failure to comply with this law implies that the offender is "too good for his company"; and this, on the road, is the unpardonable sin. The Englishman "passed the time o' day" in due and ample form. "Ha! Ha!" said the gentleman with the bag. "Isn't this a sweet place? There ain't no ticca-gharries, and there ain't nothing to eat, if you haven't brought your vittles, an' they charge you three-eight for a bottle of whisky. An' Encore at that! Oh! It's a sweet place." Here he skipped about the verandah and puffed. Then turning upon the Englishman, he said fiercely:—"What have you come here for?" Now this was rude, because the ordinary form of salutation on the road is usually:—"And what are you for?" meaning, "what house do you represent?" The Englishman answered dolefully that he was travelling for pleasure, which simple explanation offended the little man with the courier-bag. He snapped his joints more excruciatingly than ever:—"For pleasure! My God! For pleasure! Come here an' wait five weeks for your money, an' mark what I'm tellin' you now, you don't get it then! But per'aps your ideas of pleasure is different from most peoples'. For pleasure! Yah!" He skipped across the sand towards the station, for he was going back with the down train, and vanished in a whirlwind of luggage and the fluttering of female skirts: in Jodhpur women are baggage-coolies. A level, drawling voice spoke from an inner room:—'E's a bit upset. That's what 'e is! I remember when I was at Gworlior" —the rest of the story was lost, and the Englishman set to work to discover the nakedness of the dak-bungalow. For reasons which do not concern the public, it is made as bitterly uncomfortable as possible. The food is infamous, and the charges seem to be wilfully pitched about eighty per cent. above the tariff, so that some portion of the bill, at least, may be paid without bloodshed, or the unseemly defilement of walls with the contents of drinking-glasses. This is short-sighted policy, and it would, perhaps, be better to lower the prices and hide the tariff, and put a guard about the house to prevent jackal-molested donkeys from stampeding into the verandahs. But these be details. Jodhpur dak-bungalow is a merry, merry place, and any writer in search of new ground to locate a madly improbable story in, could not do better than study it diligently. In front lies sand, riddled with innumerable ant-holes, and, beyond the sand, the red sandstone wall of the city, and the Mahomedan burying-ground that fringes it. Fragments of sandstone set on end mark the resting places of the faithful who are of no great account here. Above everything, a mark for miles round, towers the dun-red piles of the Fort which is also a Palace. This is set upon sandstone rock whose sharper features have been worn smooth by the wash of the windblown sand. It is as monstrous as anything in Dore's illustrations of the *Contes Drolatiques* and, wherever it wanders, the eye comes back at last to its fantastic bulk. There is no greenery on the rock, nothing but fierce sunlight or black shadow. A line of red hills forms the background of the city, and this is as bare as the picked bones of camels that lie bleaching on the sand below.

Wherever the eye falls, it sees a camel or a string of camels—lean, racer-built *sowarri* camels, or heavy, black, shag-haired trading-ships bent on their way to the Railway Station. Through the night the air is alive with the bubbling and howling of the brutes, who assuredly must suffer from nightmare. In the morning the chorus round the station is deafening. A camel has as wide a range of speech as an elephant. The Englishman found a little one, crooning happily to itself, all alone on the sands. Its nose-string was smashed. Hence its joy. But a big man left the station and beat it on the neck with a seven-foot stick, and it rose up and sobbed.

Knowing what these camels meant, but trusting nevertheless that the road would not be *very* bad, the Englishman went into the city, left a well-kunkered road, turned through a sand-worn, red sandstone gate, and sunk ankle-deep in fine reddish white sand. This was the main thoroughfare of the city. Two tame lynxes shared it with a donkey; and the rest of the population seemed to have gone to bed. In the hot weather, between ten in the morning and four in the afternoon all Jodhpur stays at home for fear of death by sunstroke, and it is possible that the habit extends far into what is officially called the "cold weather"; or, perhaps, being brought up among sands, men do not care to tramp them for pleasure. The city internally is a walled and secret place; each courtyard being hidden from view by a red sandstone wall, except in a few streets where the shops are poor and mean.

In an old house now used for the storing of tents, Akbar's mother lay two months, before the "Guardian of Mankind" was born, drawing breath for her flight to Umarkot across the desert. Seeing this place, the Englishman thought of many things not worth the putting down on paper, and went on till the sand grew deeper and deeper, and a great camel, heavily laden with stone, came round a corner and nearly stepped on him. As the evening drew on, the city woke up, and the goats and the camels and the kine came in by hundreds, and men said that wild pig, which are strictly preserved by the Princes for their own sport, were in the habit of wandering about the roads. Now if they do this in the capital, what damage must they not do to the crops in the district? Men said that they did a very great deal of damage, and it was hard to keep their noses out of anything they took a fancy to. On the evening of the Englishman's visit, the Maharaja went out, as is his laudable custom, alone and unattended, to a road actually *in* the city along which one specially big pig was in the habit of passing. His Highness got his game with a single shot behind the shoulder, and in a few days it will be pickled and sent off to the Maharana of Udaipur, as a love-gift, on account of the latter's investiture. There is great friendship between Jodhpur and Udaipur, and the idea of one King going abroad to shoot game for another has something very pretty and quaint in it.

Night fell and the Englishman became aware that the conservancy of Jodhpur might be vastly improved. Strong stenches, say the doctors, are of no importance; but there came upon every breath of heated air—and in Jodhpur City the air is warm in mid-winter—the faint, sweet, sickly, reek that one has always been taught to consider specially deadly. A few months ago there was an impressive outbreak of cholera in Jodhpur, and the Residency Doctor, who really hoped that the people would be brought to see sense, did his best to bring forward a general cleansing-scheme. But the city fathers would have none of it. Their fathers had been trying to poison themselves in well-defined ways for an indefinite number of years; and they were not going to have any of the Sahib's "sweeper nonsense."

To clinch everything, one travelled member of the community rose in his place and said:—"Why, I've been to Simla. Yes, to Simla! And even I don't want it!" This compliment should be engrossed in the archives of the Simla Municipality. Sanitation on English lines is not yet acceptable to Jodhpur.

When the black dusk had shut down, the Englishman climbed up a little hill and saw the stars come out and shine over the desert. Very far away, some camel-drivers had lighted a fire and were singing as they sat by the side of their beasts. Sound travels as far over sand as over water, and their voices came into the city wall and beat against it in multiplied echoes.

Then he returned to the House of Strange Stories—the Dak-Bungalow—and passed the time o' day to the genial, light-hearted bagman —a Cockney, in whose heart there was no thought of India, though he had travelled for years throughout the length and breadth of the Empire and over New Burma as well. There was a fort in Jodhpur, but you see that was not in his line of business exactly, and there were stables, but "you may take my word for it, them who has much to do with horses is a bad lot. You get hold of the Maharaja's coachman and he'll drive you all round the shop. I'm only waiting here collecting money." Jodhpur dak-bungalow seems to be full of men "waiting here." They lie in long chairs in the verandah and tell each other interminable stories, or stare citywards and express their opinion of some dilatory debtor in language punctuated by free spitting. They are all waiting for something; and they vary the monotony of a life they make wilfully dull beyond words, by waging war with the dak-bungalow khansama. Then they return to their long chairs, or their couches, and sleep. Some of them, in old days, used to wait as long as six weeks—six weeks in May, when the sixty miles from Marwar Junction to Jodhpur was covered in three days by slow-pacing bullock carts! Some of them are bagmen, able to describe the demerits of every dak-bungalow from the Peshin to Pagan, and southward to Hyderabad—men of substance who have "The Trades" at their back. It is a terrible thing to be in "The Trades," that great Doomsday Book of Calcutta, in whose pages are written the names of doubtful debtors. Let light-hearted purchasers take note.

And the others, who wait and swear and spit and exchange anecdotes—what are they? Bummers, land-sharks, skirmishers for their bread. It would be cruel in a fellow-tramp to call them loafers. Their lien upon the State may have its origin in horses, or anything else; for the State buys anything vendible, from Abdul Raymon's most promising importations to—a patent, self-acting corkscrew. They are a mixed crew, but amusing and full of strange stories of adventure by land and by sea. And their ends are as curiously brutal as their lives. A wanderer was once swept into the great, still backwater that divides the loaferdom of Upper India—that is to say, Calcutta and Bombay—from the north-going current of Madras, where Nym and Pistol are highly finished articles with certificates. This backwater is a dangerous place to break down in, as the men on the road know well. "You can run Rajputana in a pair o' sack breeches an' an old hat, but go to Central Injia with pice," says the wisdom of the road. So the waif died in the bazaar, and the Barrack-master Sahib gave orders for his burial. It might have been the bazaar sergeant, or it might have been an hireling who was charged with the disposal of the body. At any rate, it was an Irishman who said to the Barrack-master Sahib:—"Fwhat about that loafer?" "Well, what's the matter?" "I'm considtherin whether I'm to mash in his thick head, or to break his long legs. He won't fit the storecoffin anyways."

Here the story ends. It may be an old one; but it struck the Englishman as being rather unsympathetic in its nature; and he has preserved it for this reason. Were the Englishman a mere Secretary of State instead of an enviable and unshackled vagabond, he would remodel that Philanthropic Institution for Teaching Young Subalterns how to Spell—variously called the Intelligence and the Political Department—and giving each *omedwar* the pair of sack breeches and old hat, above prescribed, would send him out for a twelvemonth on the road. Not that he might learn to swear Australian oaths (which are superior to any ones in the market) or to drink bazaar-drinks (which are very bad indeed), but in order that he might gain an insight into the tertiary politics of States—things less imposing than succession-cases and less wearisome than boundary disputes, but—here speaks Ferdinand Count Fathom, in an Intermediate compartment, very drunk and very happy—"Worth knowing a little—Oh no! Not at all."

A small volume might be written of the ways and the tales of Indian loafers of the more brilliant order—such Chevaliers of the Order of Industry as would throw their glasses in your face did you call them loafers. They are a genial, blasphemous, blustering crew, and pre-eminent even in a land of liars.

XIII.

A King's House and Country. Further Consideration of the Hat-marked Caste.

THE hospitality that spreads tables in the wilderness, and shifts the stranger from the back of the hired camel into the two-horse victoria, must be experienced to be appreciated.

To those unacquainted with the peculiarities of the native-trained horse, this advice may be worth something. Sit as far back as ever you can, and, if Oriental courtesy have put an English bit and bridoon in a mouth by education intended for a spiked curb, leave the whole contraption alone. Once acquainted with the comparative smoothness of English ironmongery, your mount will grow frivolous. In which event a four-pound steeplechase saddle, accepted through sheer shame, offers the very smallest amount of purchase to untrained legs.

The Englishman rode up to the Fort, and by the way learnt all these things and many more. He was provided with a racking, female, horse who swept the gullies of the city by dancing sideways.

The road to the Fort which stands on the Hill of Strife, wound in and out of sixty-foot hills, with a skilful avoidance of all shade; and this was at high noon, when puffs of heated air blew from the rocks on all sides. "What must the heat be in May?" The Englishman's companion was a cheery Brahmin, who wore the lightest of turbans and sat the smallest of neat little country-breds. "Awful!" said the Brahmin. "But not so bad as in the district. Look there!" and he pointed from the brow of a bad eminence, across the quivering heat-haze, to where the white sand faded into bleach blue sky, and the horizon was shaken and tremulous. "It's very bad in summer. Would knock you—Oh yes—all to smash, but we are accustomed to it." A rock-strewn hill, about half a mile, as the crow flies, from the Fort was pointed out as the place whence, at the beginning of this century, the Pretender Sowae besieged Raja Maun for five months, but could make no headway against his foe. One gun of the enemy's batteries specially galled the Fort, and the Jodhpur King offered a village to any of his gunners who should dismount it. "It was smashed," said the Brahmin. "Oh yes, all to pieces." Practically, the city which lies below the Fort is indefensible, and during the many wars of Marwar has generally been taken up by the assailants without resistance.

Entering the Fort by the Jeypore Gate, and studiously refraining from opening his umbrella, the Englishman found shadow and coolth, took off his hat to the tun-bellied, trunk-nosed God of Good-Luck who had been very kind to him in his wanderings, and sat down near half-a-dozen of the Maharaja's guns bearing the mark, "A. Broome, Cossipore, 1857," or "G. Hutchinson, Cossipore, 1838." Now rock and masonry are so curiously blended in this great pile that he who walks through it loses sense of being among buildings. It is as though he walked through mountain-gorges. The stone-paved, inclined planes, and the tunnel-like passages driven under a hundred feet height of buildings, increase this impression. In many places the wall and rock runs up unbroken by any window for forty feet.

It would be a week's work to pick out even roughly the names of the dead who have added to the buildings, or to describe the bewildering multiplicity of courts and ranges of rooms; and, in the end, the result would be as satisfactory as an attempt to describe a night-mare. It is said that the rock on which the Fort stands is four miles in circuit, but no man yet has dared to estimate the size of the city that they call the Palace, or the mileage of its ways. Ever since Ras Joda, four hundred years ago, listened to the voice of a *Fogi* and leaving Mundore built his eyrie on the "Bird's Nest," as the Hill of Strife was called, the Palaces have grown and thickened. Even to-day the builders are still at work. Takht Singh, the present ruler's predecessor, built royally. An incomplete bastion and a Hall of Flowers are among the works of his pleasure. Hidden away behind a mighty wing of carved red sandstone, lie rooms set apart for Viceroys, Durbar Halls, and dinner-rooms without end. A gentle gloom covers the evidences of the catholic taste of the State in articles of "bigotry and virtue"; but there is enough light to show the *raison d'etre* of the men who wait in the dak-bungalow. And, after all, what is the use of Royalty in these days if a man may not take delight in the pride of the eye? Kumbha Rana, the great man of Chitor, fought like a Rajput, but he had an instinct which made him build the Tower of Victory at, who knows, what cost of money and life. The fighting-instinct thrown back upon itself, must have some sort of outlet; and a merciful Providence wisely ordains that the Kings of the East in the nineteenth century shall take pleasure in "shopping" on an imperial scale. Dresden China snuff-boxes, mechanical engines, electro-plated fish-slicers, musical boxes, and gilt, blownglass, Christmas-Tree balls do not go well with the splendours of a Palace that might have been built by Titans and coloured by the morning sun. But there are excuses to be made for Kings who have no work to do—at least such work as their fathers understood best.

In one of the higher bastions stands a curious specimen of one of the earliest *mitrailleuses*—a cumbrous machine carrying twenty gun-barrels in two rows, which small-arm fire is flanked by two tiny cannon. As a muzzle-loading implement its value after the first discharge would be insignificant; but the soldiers lounging by assured the Englishman that it had done good service in its time: it was eaten with rust.

A man may spend a long hour in the upper tiers of the Palaces, but still far from the roof-tops, in looking out across the desert. There are Englishmen in these wastes, who say gravely that there is nothing so fascinating as the sand of Bikanir and Marwar. "You see," explained an enthusiast of the Hat-marked Caste, "you are not shut in by roads, and you can go just as you please. And, somehow, it grows upon you as you get used to it, and you end, y'know, by falling in love with the place." Look steadily from the Palace westward where the city with its tanks and serais is spread at your feet, and you will, in a lame way, begin to understand the fascination of the desert which, by those who have felt it, is said to be even stronger than the fascination of the road. The city is of red-sandstone and dull and sombre to look at. Beyond it, where the white sand lies, the country is dotted with camels limping into the Eiwigkeit or coming from the same place. Trees appear to be strictly confined to the suburbs of the city. Very good. If you look long enough across the sands, while a voice in your ear is telling you of half-buried cities, old as old Time and wholly unvisited by Sahibs, of districts where the white man is unknown, and of the wonders of far-way Jeysulmir ruled by a half distraught king, sand-locked and now smitten by a terrible food and water famine, you will, if it happen that you are of a sedentary and civilised nature, experience a new emotion—will be conscious of a great desire to take one of the lobbing camels and get away into the desert, away from the last touch of To-day, to meet the Past face to face. Some day a novelist will exploit the unknown land from the Rann, where the wild ass breeds, northward and eastward, till he comes to the Indus. That will be when Rider Haggard has used up Africa and a new "She" is needed.

But the officials of Marwar do not call their country a desert. On the contrary, they administer it very scientifically and raise, as has been said, about thirty-eight lakhs from it. To come back from the influence and the possible use of the desert to more prosaic facts. Read quickly a rough record of things in modern Marwar. The old is drawn in Tod, who speaks the truth. The Maharaja's right-hand in the work of the State is Maharaj Sir Pertab Singh, Prime Minister, A.-D.-C. to the Prince of Wales, capable of managing the Marwari who intrigues like a—Marwari, equally capable, as has been seen, of moving in London Society, and Colonel of a newly-raised "crack" cavalry corps. The Englishman would have liked to have seen him, but he was away in the desert somewhere, either marking a boundary or looking after a succession case. Not very long ago, as the Setts of Ajmir knew well, there was a State debt of fifty lakhs. This has now been changed into a surplus of three lakhs, and the revenue is growing. Also, the simple Dacoit who used to enjoy himself very pleasantly, has been put into a department, and the Thug with him.

Consequently, for the department takes a genuine interest in this form of *shikar,* and the gaol leg-irons are not too light, dacoities have been reduced to such an extent that men say "you may send a woman, with her ornaments upon her, from Sojat to Phalodi, and she will not lose a nose-ring." Also, and this in a Rajput State is an important matter, the boundaries of nearly every village in Marwar have been demarcated, and boundary *rixes,* in which both sides preferred small-arm fire to the regulation *lathi,* are unknown. The open-handed system of giving away villages had raised a large and unmannerly crop of *jaghirdars.* These have been taken and brought in hand by Sir Pertab Singh, to the better order of the State.

A Punjabi Sirdar, Har Dyal Singh, has reformed, or made rather, Courts on the Civil and Criminal Side; and his hand is said to be found in a good many sweepings out of old corners. It must always be borne in mind that everything that has been done, was carried through over and under unlimited intrigue, for Jodhpur is a Native State. Intrigue must be met with intrigue by all except Gordons or demi-gods; and it is curious to hear how a reduction in tariff, or a smoothing out of some tangled Court, had to be worked by shift and by-way. The tales are comic, but not for publication. Howbeit! Har Dayal Singh got his training in part under the Punjab Government, and in part in a little Native State far away in the Himalayas, where the *gumnameh* was not altogether an unknown animal. To the credit of the "Pauper Province" be it said, it is not easy to circumvent a Punjabi. The details of his work would be dry reading. The result of it is good, and there is justice in Marwar, and order and firmness in its administration.

Naturally, the land- revenue is the most interesting thing in Marwar from an administrative point of view. The basis of it is a tank about the size of a swimming-bath, with a catchment of several hundred square yards, draining through leeped channels. When God sends the rain, the people of the village drink from the tank. When the rains fail, as they failed this year, they take to their wells, which are brackish and breed guinea-worm. For these reasons the revenue, like the Republic of San Domingo, is never alike for two years running. There are no canal questions to harry the authorities; but the fluctuations are enormous. Under the Aravalis the soil is good: further north they grow millet and pasture cattle, though, said a Revenue Officer cheerfully,—"God knows what the brutes find to eat." *Apropos* of irrigation, the one canal deserves special mention, as showing how George Stephenson came to Jodhpur and astonished the inhabitants. Six miles from the city proper lies the Balsamand Sagar, a great tank. In the hot weather, when the city tanks ran out or stank, it was the pleasant duty of the women to tramp twelve miles at the end of the day's work to fill their lotahs. In the hot weather Jodhpur is—let a simile suffice. Sukkur in June would be Simla to Jodhpur.

The State Engineer, who is also the Jodhpur State Line, for he has no European subordinates, conceived the idea of bringing the water from the Balsamand into the city. Was the city grateful? Not in the least. It said that the Sahib wanted the water to run uphill and was throwing money into the tank. Being true Marwaris, men betted on the subject. The canal—a built out one, for water must not touch earth in these parts—was made at a cost of something over a lakh, and the water came down because the tank was a trifle higher than the city. Now, in the hot weather, the women need not go for long walks, but the Marwari cannot understand how it was that the "waters came down to Jodhpur." From the Marwari to money matters is an easy step. Formerly, that is to say up to within a very short time, the Treasury of Jodhpur was conducted in a shiftless, happy-go-lucky sort of fashion not uncommon in Native States, whereby the Mahajuns "held the bag" and made unholy profits on discount and other things, to the confusion of the Durbar Funds and their own enrichment. There is now a Treasury modelled on English lines, and English in the important particular that money is not to be got from it for the asking, and the items of expenditure are strictly looked after.

In the middle of all this bustle of reform planned, achieved, frustrated and re-planned, and the never-ending underground warfare that surges in a Native State, moved the English officers—the irreducible minimum of exiles. As a caste, the working Englishmen in Native States are curiously interesting; and the traveller whose tact by this time has been Wilfred-blunted by tramping, sits in judgment upon them as he has seen them. In the first place, they are, they must be, the fittest who have survived; for though, here and there, you shall find one chafing bitterly against the burden of his life in the wilderness, one to be pitied more than any chained beast, the bulk of the caste are honestly and unaffectedly fond of their work, fond of the country around them, and fond of the people they deal with. In each State their answer to a certain question is the same. The men with whom they are in contact are "all right when you know them, but you've got to know them first" as the music-hall song says. Their hands are full of work; so full that, when the incult wanderer said—"What do you find to do?" they looked upon him with contempt and amazement—exactly as the wanderer himself had once looked upon a Globe-Trotter, who had put to him the same impertinent query. And—but here the Englishman may be wrong —it seemed to him that in one respect their lives were a good deal more restful and concentrated than those of their brethren under the British Government. There was no talk of shiftings and transfers and promotions, stretching across a Province and a half, and no man said anything about Simla. To one who has hitherto believed that Simla is the hub of the Empire, it is disconcerting to hear:—"O Simla! That's where you Bengalis go. We haven't anything to do with Simla down here." And no more they have. Their talk and their interests run in the boundaries of the States they serve, and, most striking of all, the gossipy element seems to be cut out altogether. It is a backwater of the river of Anglo-Indian life—or is it the main current, the broad stream that supplies the motive power, and is the other life only the noisy ripple on the surface? You who have lived, not merely looked at, both lives, decide. Much can be learnt from the talk of the caste—many curious, many amusing, and some startling things. One hears stories of men who take a poor, impoverished State as a man takes a wife, "for better or worse," and, moved by some incomprehensible ideal of virtue, consecrate—that is not too big a word—consecrate their lives to that State in all single-heartedness and purity. Such men are few, but they exist to-day, and their names are great in lands where no Englishman travels. Again the listener hears tales of grizzled diplomats of Rajputana—Machiavellis who have hoisted a powerful intriguer with his own intrigue, and bested priestly cunning, and the guile of the Oswal, simply that the way might be clear for some scheme which should put money into a tottering Treasury, or lighten the taxation of a few hundred thousand men—or both; for this can be done. One tithe of that force spent on their own advancement would have carried such men very far.

Those who know anything of the internals of government, know that such men must exist, for their works are written between the lines of the Administration Reports; but to hear about them and to have them pointed out, is quite a different thing. It breeds respect and a sense of shame and frivolity in the mind of the mere looker-on, which may be good for the soul.

Truly the Hat-marked Caste are a strange people. They are so few and so lonely and so strong. They can sit down in one place for years, and see the works of their hands and the promptings of their brain, grow to actual and beneficent life, bringing good to thousands. Less fettered than the direct servant of the Indian Government, and working over a much vaster charge, they seem a bigger and a more large-minded breed. And that is saying a good deal.

But let the others, the little people bound down and supervised, and strictly limited and income-taxed, always remember that the Hat-marked are very badly off for shops. If they want a necktie they must get it up from Bombay, and in the rains they can hardly move about; and they have no amusements and must go a day's railway journey for a rubber, and their drinking water is doubtful; and there is rather less than one lady *per* ten thousand square miles.

After all, comparative civilisation has its advantages.

XIV.

Among the Houyhnhnmns.

JODHPUR differs from the other States of Rajputana in that its Royalty are peculiarly accessible to an inquiring public. There are wanderers, the desire of whose life it is "to see Nabobs," which is the Globe-trotter's title for any one in unusually clean clothes, or an Oudh Taluqdar in gala dress. Men asked in Jodhpur whether the Englishman would like to see His Highness. The Englishman had a great desire to do so, if His Highness would be in no way inconvenienced. Then they scoffed:— "Oh, he won't *durbar* you, you needn't flatter yourself. If he's in the humour he'll receive you like an English country-gentleman." How in the world could the owner of such a place as Jodhpur Palace be in any way like an English country-gentleman? The Englishman had not long to wait in doubt. His Highness intimated his readiness to see the Englishman between eight and nine in the morning at the Raika-Bagh. The Raika-Bagh is not a Palace, for the lower storey and all the detached buildings round it are filled with horses. Nor can it in any way be called a stable, because the upper storey contains sumptuous apartments full of all manner of valuables both of the East and the West. Nor is it in any sense a pleasure-garden, for it stands on soft white sand, close to a multitude of litter and sand training tracks, and is devoid of trees for the most part. Therefore the Raika-Bagh is simply the Raika-Bagh and nothing else. It is now the chosen residence of the Maharaja who loves to live among his four hundred or more horses. All Jodhpur is horse-mad by the way, and it behoves anyone who wishes to be anyone, to keep his own race-course. The Englishman went to the Raika-Bagh, which stands half a mile or so from the city, and passing through a long room filled with saddles by the dozen, bridles by the score, and bits by the hundred, was aware of a very small and lively little cherub on the roof of a garden-house. He was carefully muffled, for the morning was chill. "Good morning," he cried cheerfully in English, waving a mittened hand. "Are you going to see my faver and the horses?" It was the Maharaj Kanwar, the Crown Prince, the apple of the Maharaja's eye, and one of the quaintest little bodies that ever set an Englishman disrespectfully laughing. He studies English daily with one of the English officials of the State, and stands a very good chance of being thoroughly spoiled, for he is a general pet. Also, as befits his dignity, he has his own carriage or carriages, his own twelve-hand stable, his own house and retinue, and everything handsome about him.

A few steps further on, in a little enclosure in front of a small two-storeyed white bungalow, sat His Highness the Maharaja, deep in discussion with the State Engineer. He wore an English ulster, and within ten paces of him was the first of a long range of stalls. There was an informality of procedure about Jodhpur which, after the strained etiquette of other States, was very refreshing. The State Engineer, who has a growing line to attend to, cantered away, and His Highness after a few introductory words, knowing what the Englishman would be after, said:—"Come along, and look at the horses." Other formality there was absolutely none. Even the indispensable knot of hangers-on stood at a distance, and behind a paling, in this most rustic country residence. A well-bred fox-terrier took command of the proceedings, after the manner of dogs all the world over, and the Maharaja led to the horse-boxes. But a man turned up, bending under the weight of much bacon. "Oh! here's the pig I shot for Udaipur last night. You see that is the best piece. It's pickled, and that's what makes it yellow to look at." He patted the great side that was held up. "There will be a camel sowar to meet it half way to Udaipur; and I hope Udaipur will be pleased with it. It was a very big pig." "And where did you shoot it, Maharaja Sahib?" "Here," said His Highness, smiting himself high up under the armpit. "Where else would you have it?" Certainly this descendant of Raja Maun was more like an English country-gentleman than the Englishman in his ignorance had deemed possible. He led on from horse-box to horse-box, the terrier at his heels, pointing out each horse of note; and Jodhpur has many. "There's *Raja,* twice winner of the Civil Service Cup." The Englishman looked reverently, and *Raja* rewarded his curiosity with a vicious snap, for he was being dressed over, and his temper was out of joint. Close to him stood *Autocrat,* the grey with the nutmeg marks on the off-shoulder, a picture of a horse, also disturbed in his mind. Next to him was a chestnut Arab, a hopeless cripple, for one of his knees had been smashed and the leg was doubled up under him. It was *Turquoise,* who, six or eight years ago, rewarded good feeding by getting away from his *sais,* falling down and ruining himself, but who, none the less, has lived an honoured pensioner on the Maharaja's bounty ever since. No horses are shot in the Jodhpur stables, and when one dies—they have lost not more than twenty-five in six years—his funeral is an event. He is wrapped in a white sheet which is strewn with flowers, and, amid the weeping of the *saises,* is borne away to the burial ground.

After doing the honours for nearly half an hour the Maharaja departed, and as the Englishman has not seen more than forty horses, he felt justified in demanding more. And he got them. *Eclipse* and *Young Revenge* were out down-country, but *Sherwood,* at the stud, *Shere Ali, Conqueror, Tynedale, Sherwood II.,* a maiden of Abdul Rahman's, and many others of note, were in, and were brought out. Among the veterans, a wrathful, rampant, red horse still, came *Brian Boru,* whose name has been written large in the chronicles of the Indian turf, jerking his *sais* across the road. His near fore is altogether gone, but as a pensioner he condescends to go in harness, and is then said to be a "handful." He certainly looks it.

At the two hundred and fifty-seventh horse, and perhaps the twentieth block of stables, the

Englishman's brain began to reel, and he demanded rest and information on a certain point. He had gone into some fifty stalls, and looked into all the rest, and in the looking had searchingly sniffed. But, as truly as he was then standing far below *Brian Boru's* bony withers, never the ghost of a stench had polluted the keen morning air. This City of the Houyhnhnmns was specklessly clean—cleaner than any stable, racing or private, that he had been into. How was it done? The pure white sand accounted for a good deal, and the rest was explained by one of the Masters of Horse:—"Each horse has one *sais* at least—old *Ringwood* he had four —and we make 'em work. If we didn't we'd be mucked up to the horses' bellies in no time. Everything is cleaned off at once; and whenever the sand's tainted it's renewed. There's quite enough sand you see hereabouts. Of course we can't keep their coats so good as in other stables, by reason of the rolling; but we can keep 'em pretty clean."

To the eye of one who knew less than nothing about horse-flesh, this immaculate purity was very striking, and quite as impressive was the condition of the horses, which was English—quite English. Naturally, none of them were in any sort of training beyond daily exercise, but they were fit and in such thoroughly good fettle. Many of them were out on the various tracks, and many were coming in. Roughly, two hundred go out of a morning, and it is to be feared, learn from the heavy going of the Jodhpur courses, how to hang in their stride. This is a matter for those who know, but it struck the Englishman that a good deal of the unsatisfactory performances of the Jodhpur stables might be accounted for by their having lost the clean stride on the sand, and having to pick it up gradually on the less holding down-country courses—unfortunately when they were *not* doing training gallops, but the real thing. This small theory is given for instant contradiction by those who understand.

It was pleasant to sit down and watch the rush of the horses through the great opening—gates are not affected—going on to the countryside where they take the air. Here a boisterous, unschooled Arab shot out across the road and cried "Ha! Ha!" in the scriptural manner, before trying to rid himself of the grinning black imp on his back. Behind him a Cabuli—surely all Cabulis must have been born with Pelhams in their mouths—bored sulkily across the road, or threw himself across the path of a tall, mild-eyed Kurnal-bred youngster, whose cocked ears and swinging head showed that, though he was so sedate, he was thoroughly taking in his surroundings, and would very much like to know if there were anybody better than himself on the course that morning. Impetuous as a school-boy and irresponsible as a monkey, one of the Prince's polo ponies, not above racing in his own set, would answer the query by rioting past the pupil of Parrott, the monogram on his body-cloth flapping free in the wind, and his head and hogged tail in the elements as Uncle Remus hath it. The youngster would swing himself round, and polka-mazurka for a few paces, till his attention would be caught by some dainty Child of the Desert, fresh from the Bombay stables, sweating at every sound, backing and filling like a rudderless ship. Then, thanking his stars that he was wiser than some people, number 177 would lob on to the track and settle down to his spin like the gentleman he was. Elsewhere, the eye fell upon a cloud of nameless ones, purchases from Abdul Rahman, whose worth will be proved next hot weather, when they are seriously taken in hand—skirmishing over the face of the land and enjoying themselves immensely. High above everything else, like a collier among barges, screaming shrilly, a black, flamboyant Marwari stallion with a crest like the crest of a barb, barrel-bellied, goose-rumped and river-maned, pranced through the press, while the slow-pacing waler carriage-horses eyed him with deep disfavour, and the Maharaj Kanwar's tiny mount capered under his pink, roman nose, kicking up as much dust as the *Foxhall* colt who had got on to a lovely patch of sand and was dancing a saraband in it. In and out of the tangle, going down to or coming back from the courses, ran, shuffled, rocketed, plunged, sulked or stampeded countless horses of all kinds, shapes and descriptions—so that the eye at last failed to see what they were, and only retained a general impression of a whirl of bays, greys, iron greys, and chestnuts with white stockings, some as good as could be desired, others average, but not one distinctly bad.

"We have no downright bad 'uns in this stable. What's the use?" said the Master of Horse calmly. "They are all good beasts and, one with another, must cost more than a thousand each. This year's new ones bought from Bombay and the pick of our own studs, are a hundred strong about. May be more. Yes, they look all right enough; but you can never know what they are going to turn out. Live-stock is very uncertain." "And how are the stables managed: how do you make room for the fresh stock?" "Something this way. Here are all the new ones and Parrott's lot, and the English colts that Maharaja Pertab Singh brought out with him from Home. *Winterlake* out o' *Queen's Consort,* that chestnut with the two white stockings you're looking at now. Well, next hot weather we shall see what they're made of and which is who. There's so many that the trainer hardly knows 'em one from another till they begin to be a good deal forward. Those that haven't got the pace, or that the Maharaja don't fancy, they're taken out and sold for what they'll bring. The man who takes the horses out has a good job of it. He comes back and says: —'I sold such and such for so much, and here's the money!' That's all. Well, our rejections are worth having. They have taken prizes at the Poona Horse Show. See for yourself. Is there one of those there that you wouldn't be glad to take for a hack, and look well after too? Only they're no use to us, and so out they go by the score. We've got sixty riding-boys, perhaps more, and they've got their work cut out to keep them all going. What you've seen are only the stables. We've got one stud at Bellara, eighty miles out, and they come in sometimes in droves of three and four hundred from the stud. They raise Marwaris there too, but that's entirely under native management. We've got nothing to do with that. The natives reckon a Marwari the best country-bred you can lay hands on; and some of them are beauties! Crests on 'em like the top of a wave. Well there's that stud, and another stud and, reckoning one with another, I should say the Maharaja has nearer twelve hundred than a thousand horses of his own. For this place here, two wagon-loads of grass come in every day from Marwar Junction. Lord knows how many saddles and bridles we've got. I never counted. I suppose we've about forty carriages, not counting the ones that get shabby and are stacked in places in the city, as I suppose you've seen. We take 'em out in the morning, a regular string all together, brakes and all; but the prettiest turn-out we ever turned out was Lady Dufferin's pony four-in-hand. Walers—thirteen-two the wheelers I think, and thirteen-one the leaders. They took prizes at Poona. That *was* a pretty turn-out. The prettiest in India. Lady Dufferin, she drove it when the Viceroy was down here last year. There are bicycles and tricycles in the carriage department too. I don't know how many, but when the Viceroy's camp was held, there was about one a-piece for the gentlemen, with remounts. They're somewhere about the place now, if you want to see them. How do we manage to keep the horses so quiet? You'll find some o' the youngsters play the goat a good deal when they come out o' stable, but, as you say, there's no vice generally. It's this way. We don't allow any curry-combs. If we did, the *saises* would be wearing out their brushes on the combs. It's all elbow grease here. They've got to go over the horses with their hands. They must handle 'em, and a native he's afraid of a horse. Now an English groom, when the horse is doing the fool, clips him over the head with a curry-comb, or punches him in the belly; and that hurts the horse's feelings. A native, he just stands back till the trouble is over. He *must* handle the horse or he'd get into trouble for not dressing him, so it comes to all handling and no licking, and that's why you won't get hold of a really vicious brute in these stables. Old *Ringwood* he had four *saises,* and he wanted 'em every one, but the other horses haven't more than one *sais* a-piece. The Maharaja he keeps fourteen or fifteen horses for his own riding. Not that he cares to ride now, but he likes to have his horses; and no one else can touch 'em. Then there's the horse that he mounts his visitors on, when they come for pig-sticking and such like, and then there's a lot of horses that go to Maharaja Pertab Singh's new cavalry regiment. So you see a horse can go through all three degrees sometimes before he gets sold, and be a good horse at the end of it. And I think that's about all!"

A cloud of youngsters, sweating freely and ready for any mischief, shot past on their way to breakfast, and the conversation ended in a cloud of sand and the drumming of hurrying hooves.

In the Raika-Bagh are more racing cups than this memory holds the names of. Chiefest of all was the Delhi Assemblage Cup—the Imperial Vase, of solid gold, won by *Crown Prince.* The other pieces of plate were not so imposing. But of all the Crown Jewels, the most valuable appeared at the end of the inspection. It was the small Maharaj Kanwar lolling in state in a huge barouche—his toes were at least two feet off the floor—that was taking him from his morning drive. "Have you seen *my* horses?" said the Maharaj Kanwar. The four twelve-hand ponies had been duly looked over, and the future ruler of Jodhpur departed satisfied.

XV.

Treats of the Startling Effect of a reduction in Wages and the Pleasures of Loaferdom. Paints the State of the Boondi Road and the Treachery of Ganesh of Situr.

"A TWENTY-FIVE per cent. reduction all roun' an' no certain leave when you wants it. *Of* course the best men goes somewhere else. That's only natural, and 'eres this sanguinary down mail a stickin' in the eye of the Khundwa down! I tell you, Sir, India's a bad place—a very bad place. 'Tisn't what it was when I came out one and thirty years ago, an' the drivers was getting their seven and eight 'undred rupees a month an' was treated as *men.*"

The Englishman was on his way to Nasirabad, and a gentleman in the Railway was explaining to him the real reason of the decadence of the Empire. It was because the Rajputana-Malwa Railway had cut all its employes twenty-five per cent. And, in truth, there is a good deal of fine free language where gentlemen in the carriage department, foremen-fitters, station and assistant stationmasters do foregather. It is ungenerous to judge a caste by a few samples; but the Englishman had on the road and elsewhere seen a good deal of gentlemen on the Railway, and is prepared to write down here that they spend their pay in a manner that would do credit to an income of a thousand a month. Now they are saying that the twenty-five per cent. reduction is depriving them of the pleasures of life. So much the better if it makes them moderately economical in their expenditure. Revolving these things in his mind, together with one or two stories of extravagance not quite fit for publication, the Englishman came to Nasirabad, before sunrise, and there to a tonga. Imagine an icy pause of several minutes followed by language. Quoth Ram Baksh, proprietor, driver, *sais,* and everything else, calmly:—"At this time of the year and having regard to the heat of the sun who wants a top to a tonga? I have no top. I have a top, but it would take till twelve o'clock to put it on. And behold, Sahib, Padre Martum Sahib went in this tonga to Deoli. All the officer Sahibs of Deoli and Nasirabad go in this tonga, for *shikar.* This is a 'shutin-tonga!'" When Church and Army are brought against one, argument is in vain. But to take a soft, office-bred unfortunate into the wilderness, upon a skeleton, a diagram of a conveyance, is brutality. Ram Baksh did not see it, and headed his two thirteen-hand rats straight towards the morning sun, along a beautiful military road. "We shall get to Deoli in six hours," said Ram Baksh the boastful, and, even as he spoke, the spring of the tonga bar snapt "mit a harp-like melodious twang." "What does it matter?" said Ram Baksh. "Has the Sahib never seen a tonga-iron break before? Padre Martum Sahib and all the officer Sahibs in Deoli"—"Ram Baksh," said the Englishman sternly, "I am not a Padre Sahib nor an officer Sahib, and if you say anything more about Padre Martum Sahib or the officers in Deoli I shall grow very angry, and beat you with a stick, Ram Baksh."

"Humph," said Ram Baksh, "I knew you were not a Padre Sahib." The little mishap was patched up with string, and the tonga went on merrily. It is Stevenson who says that the "invitation to the road," nature's great morning song, has not yet been properly understood or put to music. The first note of it is the sound of the dawn-wind through long grass, and the last, in this country, the creaking of the bullock wains getting under way in some unseen *serai*. It is good, good beyond expression, to see the sun rise upon a strange land and to know that you have only to go forward and possess that land—that it will dower you before the day is ended with a hundred new impressions and, perhaps, one idea. It is good to snuff the wind when it comes in over grassy uplands or down from the tops of the blue Aravalis—dry and keen as a new-ground sword. Best of all is to light the First Pipe—is there any tobacco so good as that we burn in honour of the breaking day?—and, while the ponies wake the long white road with their hooves and the birds go abroad in companies together, to thank your stars that you are neither the Subaltern who has Orderly Room, the 'Stunt who has *kacherri,* or the Judge who has Court to attend; but are only a loafer in a flannel shirt, bound, if God please, to "Little Boondi," somewhere beyond the faint hills across the plain.

But there was alloy in this delight. Men had told the Englishman darkly that Boondi State had no love for Englishmen, that there was nowhere to stop, and that no one would do anything for money. Love was out of the question. Further, it was an acknowledged fact that there were no Englishmen of any kind in Boondi. But the Englishman trusted that Ganesh would be good to him, and that he would, somehow or other, fall upon his feet as he had fallen before.

The road from Nasirabad to Deoli, being military in its nature, is nearly as straight as a ruler and about as smooth. It runs for the most part through "Arthurian" country, just such a land as the Knights of the Round Table went a-looting in—is gently sloping pasture ground, where a man could see his enemy a long way off and "ride a wallop" at him, as the Morte D'Arthur puts it, of a clear half mile. Here and there little rocky hills, the last off-shoots of the Aravalis to the west, break the ground; but the bulk of it is fair and without pimples. The Deoli Force are apparently so utterly Irregular that they can do without a telegraph, have their mails carried by runners, and dispense with bridges over all the fifty-six miles that separate them from Nasirabad. However, a man who goes shikarring for any length of time in one of Ram Baksh's tongas would soon learn to dispense with anything and everything. "All the Sahibs use my tongas; I've got eight of them and twenty pairs of horses," said Ram Baksh. "They go as far as Gangra, where the tigers are, for they are 'shutin-tongas.'" Now the Englishman knew Gangra slightly, having seen it on the way to Udaipur; and it was as perverse and rocky a place as any man would desire to see. He politely expressed doubt. "I tell you my tongas go anywhere," said Ram Baksh testily. A hay-waggon—they cut and stack their hay in these parts—blocked the road. Ram Baksh ran the tonga to one side, into a rut, fetched up on a tree-stump, rebounded on to a rock, and struck the kunkur. "Observe," said Ram Baksh; "but that is nothing. You wait till we get on the Boondi road and I'll make you shake, shake like a *botal*." "Is it *very* bad?" "I've never been to Boondi myself, but I hear it is all rocks—great rocks as big as the tonga." But though he boasted of himself and his horses nearly all the way, he could not reach Deoli in anything like the time he had set forth. "If I am not at Boondi by four," he had said, at six in the morning, "let me go without my fare." But by midday he was still far from Deoli, and Boondi lay twenty-eight miles beyond that station. "What can I do?" said he. "I've laid out lots of horses—any amount. But the fact is I've never been to Boondi. I shan't go there in the night." Ram Baksh's "lots of horses" were three pair between Nasirabad and Deoli—three pair of undersized ponies who did wonders. One place, after he had quitted a cotton waggon, a drove of *Bunjaras* and a man on horseback, with his carbine across his saddle-bow, the Englishman came to a stretch of road, so utterly desolate that he said:—" Now I am clear of everybody who ever knew me. This is the beginning of the waste into which the scape-goat was sent."

From a bush by the road side sprang up a fat man who cried aloud in English:—" How does Your Honour do? I met Your Honour in Simla this year! Are you quite well? Ya-as, I am here. Your Honour remembers me? I am travelling. Ya-as. Ha! Ha!" and he went on, leaving His Honour bemazed. It was a Babu—a Simla Babu, of that there could be no doubt; but who he was or what he was doing, thirty miles from anywhere, His Honour could not make out. The native moves about more than most folk, except railway people, imagine. The big banking firms of Upper India naturally keep in close touch with their great change-houses in Ajmir, despatching and receiving messengers regularly. So it comes to pass that the necessitous circumstances of Lieutenant Mc-Rannamack, of the Tyneside Tail-twisters, quartered on the Frontier, are thoroughly known and discussed, a thousand miles south of the cantonment where the light-hearted Lieutenant goes to the " beastly *shroff*."

This is by the way. Let us return to the banks of the Banas river, where " poor Carey," as Tod calls him, came when he was sickening for his last illness. The Banas is one of those streams which runs "over golden sands with feet of silver," but, from the scarp of its banks, Deoli in the rains must be isolated. Ram Baksh, questioned hereon, vowed that all the Officer Sahibs never dreamed of halting, but went over in boats or on elephants. According to Ram Baksh the men of Deoli must be wonderful creatures. They do nothing but use his tongas. A break in some low hills give on to the dead flat plain in which Deoli stands. "You must stop here for the night," said Ram Baksh. "I will not take my horses forward in the dark; God knows where the dak-bungalow is. I've forgotten, but any one of the Officer Sahibs in Deoli will tell you." Those in search of a new emotion would do well to run about an apparently empty cantonment, in a disgraceful shooting-tonga, in search of a place to sleep in. Chaprassis come out of the back verandahs, and are rude, and regimental Babus hop out of godowns and are flippant, while in the distance a Sahib looks out of his room, where he has evidently been sleeping, and eyes the dusty forlorn-hope with silent contempt. It should be mentioned that the dust on the Deoli road not only powders but masks the face and raiment of the passenger.

Next morning Ram Baksh was awake with the dawn, and clamorous to go on to Boondi. "I've sent a pair of horses, big horses, out there and the *sais* is a fool. Perhaps they will be lost, I want to find them." He dragged his unhappy passenger on to the road once more and demanded of all who passed the dak-bungalow which was the way to Boondi. "Observe!" said he, "there can be only one road, and if I hit it we are all right, and I'll show you what the tonga can do." "Amen," said the Englishman devoutly, as the tonga jumped into and out of a larger hole. "Without doubt this is the Boondi road," said Ram Baksh; "it is so bad."

Beyond Deoli the cultivated land gave place to more hills peppered with stones, stretches of *ak*-scrub and clumps of thorn varied with a little jhil here and there for the benefit of the officers of the Deoli Irregular Force.

It has been before said that the Boondi State has no great love for Sahibs. The state of the road proves it. "This," said Ram Baksh, tapping the wheel to see whether the last plunge had smashed a spoke, "is a very good road. You wait till you see what is ahead." And the funeral staggered on—over irrigation cuts, through buffalo wallows, and dried pools stamped with the hundred feet of kine (this by the way is the most cruel road of all), up rough banks where the rock ledges peered out of the dust, down step-cut dips ornamented with large stones, and along two-feet deep ruts of the rains, where the tonga went slantwise even to the verge of upsetting. It was a royal road—a native road—a Raj road of the roughest, and, through all its jolts and bangs and bumps and dips and heaves, the eye of Ram Baksh rolled in its blood-shot socket, seeking for the "big horses" he had so rashly sent into the wilderness. The ponies that had done the last twenty miles into Deoli were nearly used up, and did their best to lie down in the dry beds of nullahs. [*Nota bene.*—There was an unbridged nullah every five minutes, for the set of the country was towards the Mej river. In the rains it must be utterly impassable.]

A man came by on horseback, his servant walking before with platter and meal bag. "Have you seen any horses hereabouts?" cried Ram Baksh. "Horses! horses! What the Devil have I to do with your horses? D'you think I've stolen them?" Now this was decidedly a strange answer, and showed the rudeness of the land. An old woman under a tree cried out in a strange tongue and ran away. It was a dream-like experience, this hunting for horses on a "blasted heath" with neither house nor hut nor shed in sight. "If we keep to the road long enough we must find them. Look at the road! This Raj ought to be smitten with bullets." Ram Baksh had been pitched forward nearly on to the off-pony's rump, and was in a very bad temper indeed. The funeral found a house—a house walled with thorns—and near by were the two big horses, thirteen-two if an inch, and harnessed quite regardless of expense.

Everything was re-packed and re-bound with triple ropes, and the Sahib was provided with an extra cushion; but he had reached a sort of dreamsome Nirvana; having several times bitten his tongue through, cut his boot against the wheel-edge, and twisted his legs into a true-lover's-knot. There was no further sense of suffering in him. He was even beginning to enjoy himself faintly and by gasps. The road struck boldly into hills with all their teeth on edge, that is to say, their strata breaking across the road in a series of little ripples. The effect of this was amazing. The tonga skipped merrily as a young fawn, from ridge to ridge, and never seemed to have both wheels on the ground at the same time. It shivered, it palpitated, it shook, it slid, it hopped, it waltzed, it ricochetted, it bounded like a kangaroo, it blundered like a sledge, it swayed like a top-heavy coach on a down-grade, it "kicked" like a badly coupled railway carriage, it squelched like a country-cart, it squeaked in its torment, and, lastly, it essayed to plough up the ground with its nose. After three hours of this performance, it struck a tiny little ford, set between steeply-sloping banks of white dust, where the water was clear brown and full of fish. And here a blissful halt was called under the shadow of the high bank of a tobacco field.

Would you taste one of the real pleasures of Life? Go through severe acrobatic exercises in and about a tonga for four hours; then, having eaten and drank till you can no more, sprawl, in the cool of a nullah bed with your head among the green tobacco, and your mind adrift with the one little cloud in a royally blue sky. Earth has nothing more to offer her children than this deep delight of animal well-being. There were butterflies in the tobacco—six different kinds, and a little rat came out and drank at the ford. To him succeeded the flight into Egypt. The white bank of the ford framed the picture perfectly—the Mother in blue, on a great white donkey, holding the Child in her arms, and Joseph walking beside, his hand upon the donkey's withers. By all the laws of the East, Joseph should have been riding and the Mother walking. This was an exception decreed for the Englishman's special benefit. It was very warm and very pleasant, and, somehow, the passers by the ford grew indistinct, and the nullah became a big English garden, with a cuckoo singing far down in the orchard, among the apple-blossoms. The cuckoo started the dream. He was the only real thing in it, for the garden slipped back into the water, but the cuckoo remained and called and called for all the world as though he had been a veritable English cuckoo. "Cuckoo—cuckoo—cuck;" then a pause and renewal of the cry from another quarter of the horizon. After that the ford became distasteful, so the procession was driven forward and in time plunged into what must have been a big city once, but the only inhabitants were oil-men. There were abundance of tombs here, and one carried a life-like carving in high relief of a man on horseback spearing a foot-soldier. Hard by this place the road or rut turned by great gardens, very cool and pleasant, full of tombs and black-faced monkeys who quarrelled among the tombs, and shut in from the sun by gigantic banians and mango trees. Under the trees and behind the walls, priests sat singing; and the Englishman would have enquired into what strange place he had fallen, but the men did not understand him.

Ganesh is a mean little god of circumscribed powers. He was dreaming, with a red and flushed face, under a banian tree; and the Englishman gave him four annas to arrange matters comfortably at Boondi. His priest took the four annas, but Ganesh did nothing whatever, as shall be shown later. His only excuse is that his trunk was a good deal worn, and he would have been better for some more silver leaf, but that was no fault of the Englishman.

Beyond the dead city was a jhil, full of snipe and duck, winding in and out of the hills; and beyond the jhil, hidden altogether among the hills, was Boondi. The nearer to the city the viler grew the road and the more overwhelming the curiosity of the inhabitants. But what befel at Boondi must be reserved for another chapter.

XVI.

The Comedy of Errors and the Exploitation of Boondi. The Castaway of the Dispensary and the Children of the Schools. A Consideration of the Shields of Rajasthan and other trifles.

IT is high time that a new treaty were made with Maha Rao Raja Ram Singh, Bahadur, Raja of Boondi. He keeps the third article of the old one too faithfully, which says that he "shall not enter into negotiations with anyone without the consent of the British Government." He does not negotiate at all. Arrived at Boondi Gate, the Englishman asked where he might lay his head for the night, and the Quarter Guard with one accord said:—"The Sukh Mahal, which is beyond the city," and the tonga went thither through the length of the town, of which more presently, till it arrived at a pavilion on a lake—a place of two turrets connected by an open colonnade. The "house" was open to the winds of heaven and the pigeons of the Raj; but the latter had polluted more than the first could purify. A snowy-bearded chowkidar crawled out of a place of tombs which he seemed to share with some monkeys, and threw himself into Anglo-Saxon attitudes. He was a great deal worse than Ram Baksh, for he said that all the Officer Sahibs of Deoli came to the Sukh Mahal for *shikar* and—never went away again, so pleased were they. The Sahib had brought the honour of his Presence, and he was a very old man, and without a *purwana* could do nothing. Then he fell deeply asleep without warning; and there was a pause, of one hour only, which the Englishman spent in seeing the lake. It, like the jhils on the road, wound in and out among the hills, and, on the bund side, was bounded by a hill of black rock crowned with a *chhatri* of grey stone. Below the bund was a garden as fair as eye could wish, and the shores of the lake were dotted with little temples. Given a habitable house—a mere dak-bungalow—it would be a delightful spot to rest in. Warned by some bitter experiences in the past, the Englishman knew that he was in for the demi-semi-royal or embarrassing reception, when a man, being the unwelcome guest of a paternal State, is neither allowed to pay his way and make himself comfortable, nor is he willingly entertained. When he saw a one-eyed munshi, he felt certain that Ganesh had turned upon him at last. The munshi demanded and received the *purwana*. Then he sat down and questioned the traveller exhaustively as to his character and profession. Having thoroughly satisfied himself that the visitor was in no way connected with the Government or the "Agenty Sahib Bahadur," he took no further thought of the matter; and the day began to draw in upon a grassy bund, an open work pavilion, and a disconsolate tonga.

At last the faithful servitor, who had helped to fight the Battle of the Mail Bags at Udaipur, broke his silence, and vowing that all these devil-people—not more than twelve—had only come to see the tamasha, suggested the breaking of the munshi's head. And, indeed, that seemed the only way of breaking the ice; for the munshi had in the politest possible language, put forward the suggestion that there was nothing particular to show that the Sahib who held the *purwana* had really any right to hold it. The chowkidar woke up and chaunted a weird chaunt, accompanied by the Anglo-Saxon attitudes, a new set. He was an old man, and all the Sahib-log said so, and within the pavilion were tables and chairs and lamps and bath-tubs, and everything that the heart of man could desire. Even now an enormous staff of *khalassis* were arranging all these things for the comfort of the Sahib Bahadur and Protector of the Poor, who had brought the honour and glory of his Presence all the way from Deoli. What did tables and chairs and eggs and fowls and very bright lamps matter to the Raj? He was an old man and. . . . "Who put the present Raja on the guddee?" "Lake Sahib," promptly answered the chowkidar. "I was there. That is the news of many old years." Now Tod says it was he himself who installed "Lalji the beloved" in the year 1821. The Englishman began to lose faith in the chowkidar. The munshi said nothing but followed the Englishman with his one workable eye. A merry little breeze crisped the waters of the lake, and the fish began to frolic before going to bed.

"Is nobody going to do or bring anything?" said the Englishman faintly, wondering whether the local jail would give him a bed if he killed the munshi. "I am an old man," said the chowkidar, "and because of their great respect and reverence for the Sahib in whose Presence I am only a bearer of orders and a servant awaiting them, men, many men, are bringing now *kanats* which I with my own hands will wrap, here and there, there and here, in and about the pillars of this place; and thus you, O Sahib, who have brought the honour of your Presence to the Boondi Raj over the road to Deoli, which is a *kutcha* road, will be provided with a very fine and large apartment over which I will watch while you go to kill the tigers in these hills."

By this time two youths had twisted *kanats* round some of the pillars of the colonnade, making a sort of loose-box with a two-foot air-way all round the top. There was no door, but there were unlimited windows. Into this enclosure the chowkidar heaped furniture on which many generations of pigeons had evidently been carried off by cholera, until he was entreated to desist. "What," said he scornfully, "are tables and chairs to this Raj? If six be not enough, let the Presence give an order, and twelve shall be forthcoming. Everything shall be forthcoming." Here he filled a *chirag* with kerosene oil and set it in a box upon a stick. Luckily, the oil which he poured so lavishly from a quart bottle was bad, or he would have been altogether consumed.

Night had fallen long before this magnificence was ended. The superfluous furniture—chairs for the most part—was shovelled out into the darkness and by the light of a flamboyant *chirag*—a merry wind forbade candles—the Englishman went to bed, and was lulled to sleep by the rush of the water escaping from the overflow trap and the splash of the water-turtle as he missed the evasive fish. It was a curious sight. Cats and dogs rioted about the enclosure, and a wind from the lake bellied the *kanats.* The brushwood of the hills around snapped and cracked as beasts went through it, and creatures—not jackals—made dolorous noises. On the lake it seemed that hundreds of water-birds were keeping a hotel, and that there were arrivals and departures throughout the night. The Raj insisted upon providing a guard of two sepoys, very pleasant men on four rupees a month. These said that tigers sometimes wandered about on the hills above the lake, but were most generally to be found five miles away. And the Englishman promptly dreamed that a one eyed tiger came into his tent without a *purwana.* But it was only a wild cat after all; and it fled before the shoes of civilisation.

The Sukh Mahal was completely separated from the city, and might have been a country-house. It should be mentioned that Boondi is jammed into a V-shaped gorge—the valley at the main entrance being something less than five hundred yards across. As it splays out, the thickly-packed houses follow its line, and, seen from above, seem like cattle being herded together preparatory to a stampede through the gate. Owing to the set of the hills, very little of the city is visible except from the Palace. It was in search of this latter that the Englishman went abroad and became so interested in the streets that he forgot all about it for a time. Jeypore is a show-city and is decently drained; Udaipur is blessed with a State Engineer and a printed form of Government; for Jodhpur the dry sand, the burning sun, and an energetic doctor have done a good deal, but Boondi has none of these things. The crampedness of the locality aggravates the evil, and it can only be in the rains which channel and furrow the rocky hill-sides that Boondi is at all swept out. The Nal Sagar, a lovely little stretch of water, takes up the head of the valley called the Banda Gorge, and must, in the nature of things, receive a good deal of unholy drainage. But setting aside this weakness, it is a fascinating place —this jumbled city of straight streets and cool gardens, where gigantic mangoes and peepuls intertwine over gurgling water-courses, and the cuckoo comes at mid-day. It boasts no foolish Municipality to decree when a house is dangerous and unhabitable. The newer shops are built into, on to, over and under, time-blackened ruins of an older day, and the little children skip about tottering arcades and grass-grown walls, while their parents chatter below in the crowded bazaar. In the back slums, the same stones seem to be used over and over again for house-building, perhaps, because there is no space to bring up laden buffaloes. Wheeled conveyances are scarce in Boondi City—there is scant room for carts, and the streets are paved with knobsome stones, unpleasant to walk over. From time to time an inroad of *Bunjaras'* pack-bullocks sweeps the main street clear of life, or one of the Raja's elephants—he has twelve of them—blocks the way. But, for the most part, the foot passengers have all the city for their own.

They do not hurry themselves. They sit in the sun and think, or put on all the arms in the family, and, hung with ironmongery, parade before their admiring friends. Other men, lean, dark men, with bound jaws and only a tulwar for weapon, dive in and out of the dark alleys, on errands of State. It is a blissfully lazy city, doing everything in the real, true, original native way, and it is kept in very good order by the Durbar. There either is or is not an order for everything. There is no order to sell fish-ing-hooks, or to supply an Englishman with milk, or to change for him Currency Notes. He must only deal with the Durbar for whatever he requires; and wherever he goes he must be accompanied by at least two men. They will tell him nothing, for they know or affect to know nothing of the city. They will do nothing except shout at the little innocents who joyfully run after the stranger and demand *pice,* but there they are, and there they will stay till he leaves the city, accompanying him to the gate, and waiting there a little to see that he is fairly off and away. Englishmen are not encouraged in Boondi. The intending traveller would do well to take a full suit of Political uniform with the sun-flowers, and the little black sword to sit down upon. The local god is the "Agenty Sahib," and he is an incarnation without a name—at least among the lower classes. The educated, when speaking of him, always use the courtly "Bahadur" affix: and yet it is a mean thing to gird at a State which, after all, is not bound to do anything for intrusive Englishmen without any visible means of livelihood. The King of this fair city should declare the blockade absolute, and refuse to be troubled with anyone except "Colon-nel Baltah Agenty Sahib Bahadur" and the Politicals. If ever a railway is run through Kotah, as men on the Bombay side declare it must be, the cloistered glory of Boondi will depart, for Kotah is only twenty miles easterly of the city and the road is moderately good. In that day the Globe-Trotter will pry about the place, and the Charitable Dispensary—a gem among dispensaries—will be public property.

The Englishman was hunting for the statue of a horse, a great horse hight Hunja, who was a steed of Irak, and a King's gift to Rao Omeda, one time monarch of Boondi. He found it in the city square as Tod had said; and it was an unlovely statue, carven after the dropsical fashion of later Hindu art. No one seemed to know anything about it. A little further on, one cried from a bye-way in rusty English:—"Come and see my Dispensary." There are only two men in Boondi who speak English. One is the head, and the other the assistant, teacher of the English side of Boondi Free School. This third was, some twenty years ago, a pupil of the Lahore Medical College when that institution was young; and he only remembered a word here and there. He was head of the Charitable Dispensary; and insisted upon, then and there, organising a small durbar,and pulling out all his books for inspection. Escape was hopeless: nothing less than a formal inspection and introduction to all the native Baids would serve. There were sixteen beds in and about the court-yard, and between twenty and thirty out-patients stood in attendance. Making allowances for untouched Orientalism, the Dispensary is a good one, and must relieve a certain amount of human misery. There is no other in all Boondi. The operation-book, kept in English, showed the principal complaints of the country. They were:—"Asthama," "Numonia," "Skin-diseas," "Dabalaty," and "Loin-bite." This last item occurred again and again—three and four cases per week—and it was not until the Doctor said—"*Sher se mara*" that the Englishman read it aright. It was "lion-bite," or tiger, if you insist upon zoological accuracy. There was one incorrigible idiot, a handsome young man, naked as the day, who sat in the sunshine, shivering and pressing his hands to his head. "I have given him blisters and setons—have tried native and English treatment for two years, but it is no use. He is always as you see him, and now he stays here by the favour of the Durbar, which is a very good and pitiful Durbar," said the Doctor. There were many such pensioners of the Durbar—men afflicted with chronic "asthama" who stayed "by favour," and were kindly treated. They were resting in the sunshine, their hands on their knees, sure that their daily dole of grain and tobacco and opium would be forthcoming. "All folk, even little children, eat opium here," said the Doctor, and the diet-book proved it. After laborious investigation of everything, down to the last indent to Bombay for Europe medicines, the Englishman was suffered to depart. "Sir, I thank. . . ." began the Native Doctor, but the rest of the sentence stuck. Sixteen years in Boondi does not increase knowledge of English; and he went back to his patients, gravely conning over the name of the Principal of the Lahore Medical School—a College now—who had taught him all he knew, and to whom he intended to write. There was something pathetic in the man's catching at news from the outside world of men he had known as Assistant and House Surgeons who are now Rai Bahadurs, and his parade of the few shreds of English that still clung to him. May he treat "loin-bites" and "catrack" successfully for many years. In the happy, indolent, fashion that must have merits which we cannot understand, he is doing a good work, and the Durbar allows his Dispensary as much as it wants.

Close to the Dispensary stood the Free School,

and thither an importunate munshi steered the Englishman who, by this time, was beginning to persuade himself that he really was an accredited agent of Government sent to report on the progress of Boondi. From a peepul-shaded courtyard came a clamour of young voices. Thirty or forty little ones, from five to eight years old, were sitting in an open verandah learning *hissab* and Hindustani, said the teacher. No need to ask from what castes they came, for it was written on their faces that they were Mahajans, Oswals, Aggerwals, and in one or two cases it seemed, Sharawaks of Guzerat. They were learning the business of their lives and, in time, would take their fathers' places, and show in how many ways money may be manipulated. Here the profession-type came out with startling distinctness. Through the chubbiness of almost babyhood, or the delicate suppleness of mature years, in mouth and eyes and hands, it betrayed itself. The Rahtor, who comes of a fighting-stock, is a fine animal and well-bred; the Hara, who seems to be more compactly-built, is also a fine animal; but for a race that show blood in every line of their frame, from the arch of the instep to the modelling of the head, the financial—trading is too coarse a word—the financial class of Rajputana appears to be the most remarkable. Later in life many become clouded with fat on jowl and paunch; but in his youth, his quick-eyed, nimble youth, the young Marwar, to give him his business-title, is really a thing of beauty. Also his manners are courtly. The bare ground and a few slates sufficed for the children who were merely learning the ropes that drag States; but the English class, of boys from ten to twelve, was supplied with benches and forms and a table with a cloth top. The assistant teacher, for the head was on leave, was a self-taught man of Boondi, young and delicate looking, who preferred reading to speaking English. His youngsters were supplied with "The Third English Reading Book," and were painfully thumbing their way through a doggerel poem about an "old man with hoary hair." One boy, bolder than the rest, slung an English sentence at the visitor and collapsed. It was his little stock-in-trade, and the rest regarded him enviously. The Durbar supports the school, which is entirely free and open; a just distinction being maintained between the various castes. The old race prejudice against payment for knowledge came out in a reply to question.—"You must not sell teaching," said the teacher, and the class murmured applausively:—"You must not sell teaching."

The population of Boondi seems more obviously mixed than that of the other States. There are four or five thousand Mahomedans within its walls and a sprinkling of aborigines of various varieties, besides the human raffle that the Bunjaras bring in their train, with Pathans and sleek Delhi men. The new heraldry of the State is curious—something after this sort. *Or,* a demi-man, *sable,* issuant of flames, holding in right hand a sword and in the left a bow—*all proper.* In chief, a dagger of the *second,* sheathed *vest,* fessewise over seven arrows in sheaf of the *second.* This latter blazon Boondi holds in commemoration of the defeat of an Imperial Prince who rebelled against the Delhi Throne in the days of Jehangir, when Boondi, for value received, took service under the Mahomedan. It might be, but here there is no certainty, the memorial of Rao Rutton's victory over Prince Khoorm, when the latter strove to raise all Rajputana against Jehangir his father; or of a second victory over a riotous lordling who harried Mewar a little later. For this exploit, the annals say, Jehangir gave Rao Rutton honorary flags and kettle-drums which may have been melted down by the science of the Herald's College into the blazon aforesaid. All the heraldry of Rajputana is curious and, for such as hold that there is any worth in the "Royal Science," interesting. Udaipur's shield is, naturally *gules,* a sun in splendor, as befits the "children of the sun and fire," and one of the most ancient houses in India. Her crest is the straight Rajput sword, the *khanda;* for an account of the worship of which very powerful divinity read Tod. The supporters are a Bhil and a Rajput, attired for the forlorn-hope; commemorating not only the defences of Chitor, but also the connection of the great Bappa Rawul with the Bhils who even now play the principal part in the Crown-Marking of a Rana of Udaipur. Here, again, Tod explains the matter at length. Banswara claims alliance with Udaipur and carries a sun, with a label of difference of some kind. Jeypore has the five-coloured flag of Amber with a sun, because the House claim descent from Rama, and her crest is a kuchnar tree, which is the bearing of Dasaratha, father of Rama. The white horse, which faces the tiger as supporter, may or may not be the memorial of the great *aswamedha yuga* or horse sacrifice that Jey Singh, who built Jeypore, did *not* carry out.

Jodhpur has the five-coloured flag, with a falcon, in which shape Durga, the patron Goddess of the State, has been sometimes good enough to appear. She has perched in the form of a wagtail on the howdah of the Chief of Jeysulmir, whose shield is blazoned with "forts in a desert land," and a naked left arm holding a broken spear, because, the legend goes, Jeysulmir was once galled by a horse with a magic spear. They tell the story to-day, but it is a long one. The supporters of the shield—this is canting heraldry with a vengeance!—are antelopes of the desert spangled with gold coin, because the State was long the refuge of the wealthy bankers of India.

Bikanir, a younger House of Jodhpur, carries three white hawks on the five-coloured flag. The patron Goddess of Bikanir once turned the thorny jungle round the city to fruit-trees, and the crest therefore is a green tree—strange emblem for a desert principality. The motto, however, is a good one. When the greater part of the Rajput States were vassals of Akbar, and he sent them abroad to do his will, certain Princes objected to crossing the Indus, and asked Bikanir to head the mutiny because his State was the least accessible. He consented, on condition that they would all for one day greet him thus:—"*Jey Jangal dar Badshah!*" History shows what became of the objector and Bikanir's motto:—"Hail to the King of the Waste!"

proves that the tale *must* be true. But from Boondi to Bikanir is a long digression, bred by blissful idleness on the bund of the Burra. It would have been sinful not to let down a line into those crowded waters, and the Guards, who were Mahomedans, said that if the Sahib did not eat fish, they did. And the Sahib fished luxuriously, catching two and three pounders, of a perch-like build, whenever he chose to cast. He was wearied of schools and dispensaries, and the futility of heraldry accorded well with laziness—that is to say Boondi.

It should be noted, none the less, that in this part of the world the soberest mind will believe anything—believe in the ghosts by the Gow Mukh, and the dead Thakurs, who get out of their tombs and ride round the Burra Talao at Boondi—will credit every legend and lie that rises as naturally as the red flush of sunset, to gild the dead glories of Rajasthan.

XVII.

Shows that there may be Poetry in a Bank, and attempts to show the Wonders of the Palace of Boondi.

"THIS is a devil's place you have come to, Sahib. No grass for the horses, and the people don't understand anything, and their dirty pice are no good in Nasirabad. Look here!" And Ram Baksh wrathfully exhibited a handful of lumps of copper. The nuisance of taking a native out of his own beat is that he forthwith regards you not only as the author of his being, but of all his misfortunes as well. He is as hampering as a frightened child and as irritating as a man. "*Padre Martum Sahib* never came here," said Ram Baksh, with the air of one who had been led against his will into bad company.

A story about a rat that found a piece of turmeric and set up a bunnia's shop had sent the one-eyed munshi away, but a company of lesser munshis, runners and the like, were in attendance, and they said that money might be changed at the Treasury, which was in the

Palace. It was quite impossible to change it anywhere else—there was no *hookum*. From the Sukh Mahal to the Palace the road ran through the heart of the city, and by reason of the continual shouting of the munshis, not more than ten thousand of the fifty thousand people of Boondi knew for what purpose the Sahib was journeying through their midst. Cataract was the most prevalent affliction, cataract in its worst forms, and it was, therefore, necessary that men should come very close to look at the stranger. They were in no sense rude, but they stared devoutly. "He has not come for *shikar,* and he will not take petitions. He has come to see the place, and God knows what he is." The description was quite correct, as far as it went; but, somehow or another, when shouted out at four cross-ways in the midst of a very pleasant little gathering it did not seem to add to dignity or command respect.

It has been written "the *coup d'oeil* of the castellated Palace of Boondi, from whichever side you approach it, is perhaps the most striking in India. Whoever has seen the Palace of Boondi can easily picture to himself the hanging gardens of Semiramis." This is true—and more too. To give on paper any adequate idea of the Boondi-ki-Mahal is impossible. Jeypore

Palace may be called the Versailles of India; Udaipur's House of State is dwarfed by the hills round it and the spread of the Pichola lake; Jodhpur's House of Strife, grey towers on red rock, is the work of giants; but the Palace of Boondi, even in broad day-light, is such a Palace as men build for themselves in uneasy dreams—the work of goblins more than the work of men. It is built into and out of hill side, in gigantic terrace on terrace, and dominates the whole of the city. But a detailed description of it were useless. Owing to the dip of the valley in which the city stands, it can only be well seen from one place, the main road of the city; and from that point seems like an avalanche of masonry ready to rush down and whelm the gorge. Like all the other Palaces of Rajputana, it is the work of many hands, and the present Raja has thrown out a bastion of no small size on one of the lower levels, which has been four or five years in the building. Only by scaling this annex, and, from the other side of the valley, seeing how insignificant is its great bulk in the entire scheme, is it possible to get some idea of the stupendous size of the Palace. No one knows where the hill begins and where the Palace ends. Men say that there are subterranean chambers leading into the heart of the hills, and passages communicating with tne extreme limits of Taragarh, the giant fortress that crowns the hill and flanks the whole of the valley on the Palace side. They say that there is as much room under as above ground, and that none know the whole extent of the Palace. Looking at it from below, the Englishman could readily believe that nothing was impossible for those who had built it. The dominant impression was of height—height that heaved itself out of the hillside and weighed upon the eyelids of the beholder. The steep slope of the land had helped the builders in securing this effect. From the main road of the city a steep stone-paved ascent led to the first gate—name not communicated by the zealous following. Two gaudily painted fishes faced each other over the arch, and there was little except glaring colour ornamentation visible. This gate gave into what they called the *chowk* of the Palace, and one had need to look twice ere realising that this open space, crammed with human life, was a spur of the hill on which the Palace stood, paved and built over. There had been little attempt at levelling the ground. The foot-worn stones followed the contour of the ground, and ran up to the walls of the Palace smooth as glass. Immediately facing the Gate of the Fish was the

Quarter-Guard barracks, a dark and dirty room, and here, in a chamber hollowed out in a wall, were stored the big drums of State, the *nakarras*. The appearance of the Englishman seemed to be the signal for smiting the biggest of all the drums, and the dull thunder rolled up the Palace *chowk,* and came back from the unpierced Palace walls in hollow groaning. It was an eerie welcome—this single, sullen boom. In this enclosure, four hundred years ago, if the legend be true, a son of the great Rao Bando, who dreamed a dream as Pharaoh did and saved Boondi from famine, left a little band of Haras to wait his bidding while he went up into the Palace and slew his two uncles who had usurped the throne and abandoned the faith of their fathers. When he had pierced one and hacked the other, as they sat alone and unattended, he called out to his followers, who made a slaughter-house of the enclosure and cut up the usurpers' adherents. At the best of times men slip on these smooth stones; and when the place was swimming in blood, foothold must have been treacherous indeed.

An inquiry for the place of the murder of the uncles—it is marked by a staircase slab, or Tod, the accurate, is at fault—was met by the answer that the Treasury was close at hand. They speak a pagan tongue in Boondi, swallow half their words, and adulterate the remainder with local *patois*. What can be extracted from a people who call four miles variously *do kosh, do kush, dhi khas, doo-a koth,* and *diakast,* all one word ? The country-folk are quite unintelligible; which simplifies matters. It is the catching of a shadow of a meaning here and there, the hunting for directions cloaked in dialect, that is annoying. Foregoing his archæological researches, the Englishman sought the Treasury. He took careful notes; he even made a very bad drawing, but the Treasury of Boondi defied pinning down before the public. There was a gash in the brown flank of the Palace—and this gash was filled with people. A broken bees' comb with the whole hive busily at work on repairs, will give a very fair idea of this extraordinary place —the Heart of Boondi. The sunlight was very vivid without and the shadows were heavy within, so that little could be seen except this clinging mass of humanity huggling like maggots in a carcase. A stone staircase ran up to a rough verandah built out of the wall, and in the wall was a cave-like room, the guardian of whose snowy-carpeted depths was one of the refined financial classes, a man with very small hands and soft, low voice. He was girt with a sword, and held authority over the Durbar funds. He referred the Englishman courteously to another branch of the department, to find which necessitated a blundering progress up another narrow staircase crowded with loungers of all kinds. Here everything shone from constant contact of bare feet and hurrying bare shoulders. The staircase was the thing that, seen from without, had produced the bees' comb impression. At the top was a long verandah shaded from the sun, and here the Boondi Treasury worked, under the guidance of a grey-haired old man, whose sword lay by the side of his comfortably wadded cushion. He controlled twenty or thirty writers, each wrapped round a huge, country paper account-book, and each far too busy to raise his eyes.

The babble on the staircase might have been the noise of the sea so far as these men were concerned. It ebbed and flowed in regular beats, and spread out far into the courtyard below. Now and again the *click-click-click* of a scabbard tip being dragged against the wall, cut the dead sound of trampling naked feet, and a soldier would stumble up the narrow way into the sun-light. He was received, and sent back or forward by a knot of keen-eyed loungers, who seemed to act as a buffer between the peace of the Secretariat and the pandemonium of the Administrative. Saises and grass-cutters, mahouts of elephants, brokers, mahajuns, villagers from the district, and here and there a shock-headed aborigine, swelled the mob on and at the foot of the stairs. As they came up, they met the buffer-men who spoke in low voices, and appeared to filter them according to their merits. Some were sent to the far end of the verandah, where everything melted away in a fresh crowd of dark faces. Others were sent back, and joined the detachment shuffling for shoes in the *chowk.* One servant of the Palace withdrew himself to the open, underneath the verandah, and there sat yapping from time to time like a hungry dog:—"The grass! The grass! The grass!" But the men with the account-books never stirred. Other men knelt down in front of them and whispered. And they bowed their heads gravely and made entry or erasure, turning back the rustling leaves. Not often does a reach of the River of Life so present itself that it can without alteration be transferred to canvas. But the Treasury of Boondi, the view up the long verandah, stood complete and ready for any artist who cared to make it his own. And by that lighter and less malicious irony of the Fate, who is always giving nuts to those who have no teeth, the picture was clinched and brought together by a winking, brass hookah-bowl of quaint design, pitched carelessly upon a roll of dull-red cloth full in the foreground. The faces of the accountants were of pale gold, for they were an untanned breed, and the face of the old man their controller was like frosted silver.

It was a strange Treasury, but no other could have suited the Palace. The Englishman watched open-mouthed, blaming himself because he could not catch the meaning of the orders given to the flying chaprassies, nor make anything of the hum in the verandah and the tumult on the stairs. The old man took the commonplace Currency Note and announced his willingness to give change in silver. "We have no small notes here," he said. "They are not wanted. In a little while, when you next bring the Honour of your Presence this way, you shall find the silver."

The Englishman was taken down the steps and fell into the arms of a bristled giant who had left his horse in the courtyard, and the giant spoke at length, waving his arms in the air, but the Englishman could not understand him and dropped into the hub-bub at the Palace foot. Except the main lines of the building there is nothing strange or angular about it.

The rush of people seems to have rounded and softened every corner, as a river grinds down boulders. From the lowest tier, two zigzags, all of rounded stones sunk in mortar, took the Englishman to a gate where two carved elephants were thrusting at each other over the arch; and, because neither he nor any one round him could give the gate a name, he called it the "Gate of the Elephants." Here the noise from the Treasury was softened, and entry through the gate brought him into a well-known world, the drowsy peace of a King's Palace. There was a court-yard surrounded by stables, in which were kept chosen horses, and two or three *saises* were sleeping in the sun. There was no other life except the whirr and coo of the pigeons. In time—though really there is no such a thing as time off the line of railway—an official appeared begirt with the skewer-like keys that open the native bayonet-locks each from six inches to a foot long. Where was the Raj Mahal in which, sixty-six years ago, Tod formally installed Ram Singh, "who is now in his eleventh year, fair and with a lively intelligent cast of face"? The warden made no answer, but led to a room, overlooking the court-yard, in which two armed men stood before an empty throne of white marble. They motioned silently that none must pass immediately before the *takht* of the King, but go round, keeping to the far side of the double row of pillars. Near the walls were stone slabs pierced to take the butts of long, venomous, black bamboo lances; rude coffers were disposed about the room, and ruder sketches of Ganesh adorned the walls. "The men," said the warden, "watch here day and night because this place is the Rutton Daulat." That, you will concede, is lucid enough. He who does not understand it, may go to for a thick-headed barbarian.

From the Rutton Daulat the warden unlocked doors that led into a hall of audience—the Chutter Mahal—built by Raja Chutter Lal, who was killed more than two hundred years ago in the latter days of Shah Jehan for whom he fought. Two rooms, each supported on double rows of pillars, flank the open space, in the centre of which is a marble reservoir. Here the Englishman looked anxiously for some of the atrocities of the West, and was pleased to find that, with the exception of a vase of artificial flowers and a clock, both hid in *mihrabs,* there was nothing that jarred with the exquisite pillars, and the raw blaze of colour in the roofs of the rooms. In the middle of these impertinent observations, something sighed—sighed like a distressed ghost. Unaccountable voices are at all times unpleasant, especially when the hearer is some hundred feet or so above ground in an unknown Palace in an unknown land. A gust of wind had found its way through one of the latticed balconies, and had breathed upon a thin plate of metal, some astrological instrument, slung gong-wise on a tripod. The tone was as soft as that of an Aeolian harp, and, because of the surroundings, infinitely more plaintive.

There was an inlaid ivory door, set in lintel and posts crusted with looking-glass—all apparently old work. This opened into a darkened room where there were gilt and silver charpoys, and portraits, in the native fashion, of the illustrious dead of Boondi. Beyond the darkness was a balcony clinging to the sheer side of the Palace, and it was then that the Englishman realised to what a height he had climbed without knowing it. He looked down upon the bustle of the Treasury and the stream of life flowing into and out of the Gate of the Fishes where the big *nakarras* lie. Lifting his eyes, he saw how Boondi City had built itself, spreading from west to east as the confined valley became too narrow and the years more peaceable. The Boondi hills are the barrier that separates the stony, uneven ground near Deoli from the flats of Kotah, twenty miles away. From the Palace balcony the road to the eye is clear to the banks of the Chumbul river, which was the Debatable Ford in times gone by and was leaped as all rivers with any pretensions to a pedigree have been, by more than one magic horse. Northward and easterly the hills run out to Indurgarh, and southward and westerly to territory marked "disputed" on the map in the present year of grace. From this balcony the Raja can see to the limit of his territory eastward, like the good King of Yves his empire is all under his hand. He is, or the politicals err, that same Ram Singh who was installed by Tod in 1821, and for whose success in killing his first deer, Tod was, by the Queen-Mother of Boondi, bidden to rejoice. To-day the people of Boondi say:—"This Durbar is very old, so old that few men remember its beginning, for they were in our father's time." It is related also of Boondi that, on the occasion of the Queen's Jubilee, they said proudly that their ruler had reigned for sixty years, and he was a man. They saw nothing astonishing in the fact of a woman having reigned for fifty. History does not say whether they jubilated; for there are no Englishmen in Boondi to write accounts of demonstrations and foundation-stones laying to the daily newspapers, and then Boondi is very, very small. In the early morning you may see a man being pantingly chased out of the city by another man with a naked sword. This is the dak and the dak guard; and the effect is as though runner and swordsman lay under a doom—the one to fly with the fear of death always before him, as men fly in dreams, and the other to perpetually fail of his revenge. But this leaves us still in the swallow nest balcony.

The warden unlocked more doors and led the Englishman still higher, but into a garden—a heavily timbered garden with a tank for gold fish in the midst! For once the impassive following smiled when they saw that the Englishman was impressed. "This," said they, "is the Rang Bilas." "But who made it?" "Who knows? It was made long ago." The Englishman looked over the garden-wall, a foot high parapet, and shuddered. There was only the flat side of the Palace, and a drop on to the stones of the zigzags scores of feet below. Above him was the riven hillside and the decaying wall of Taragarh, and behind him this fair garden, hung like Mahomet's coffin, full of the noise of birds and the talking of the wind in the branches. The warden entered into a lengthy explanation of the nature of the delusion, showing how—but he was stopped before he had finished. His listener did not want to know "how the trick was done." Here was the garden, and there were three or four storeys climbed to reach to it. *Bus.* At one end of the garden was a small room, under treatment by native artists who were painting the panels with historical pictures, in distemper. Theirs was florid polychromatic art, but skirting the floor was a series of frescoes in red, black and white, of combats with elephants, bold and temperate as good German work. They were worn and defaced in places; but the hand of some bye-gone limner, who did not know how to waste a line, showed under the bruises and scratches, and put the newer work to shame.

Here the tour of the Palace ended; and it must be remembered that the Englishman had not gone the depth of three rooms into one flank. Acres of building lay to the right of him, and above the lines of the terraces he could see the tops of green trees. "Who knew how many gardens, such as the Rang Bilas, were to be found in the Palace?" No one answered directly, but all said that there were many. The warden gathered up his keys, and locking each door behind him as he passed, led the way down to earth. But before he had crossed the garden, the Englishman heard, deep down in the bowels of the Palace, a woman's voice singing, and the voice rang as do voices in caves. All Palaces in India excepting dead ones, such as that of Amber, are full of eyes. In some, as has been said, the idea of being watched is stronger than in others. In Boondi Palace it was overpowering —being far worse than in the green shuttered corridors of Jodhpur. There were trap-doors on the tops of terraces, and windows veiled in foliage, and bull's eyes set low in unexpected walls, and many other peep-holes and places of vantage. In the end, the Englishman looked devoutly at the floor, but when the voice of the woman came up from under his feet, he felt that there was nothing left for him but to go. Yet, excepting only this voice, there was deep silence everywhere, and nothing could be seen.

The warden returned to the Chutter Mahal to pick up a lost key. The brass table of the planets was sighing softly to itself as it swung to and fro in the wind. That was the last view of the interior of the Palace, the empty court, and the swinging sighing *jantar*.

About two hours afterwards, when he had reached the other side of the valley and seen the full extent of the buildings, the Englishman began to realise first that he had not been taken through one-tenth of the Palace; and secondly, that he would do well to measure its extent by acres, in preference to meaner measures. But what made him blush hotly, all alone among the tombs on the hill side, was the idea that he with his ridiculous demands for eggs, firewood, and sweet drinking water, should have clattered and chattered through any part of it at all.

He began to understand why Boondi does not encourage Englishmen.

XVIII.

Of the Uncivilised Night and the Departure to Things Civilised. Showing how a Friend may keep an Appointment too well.

"LET us go hence, my songs, she will not hear. Let us go hence together without fear!" But Ram Baksh the irrepressible sang it in altogether a baser key. He came by night to the pavilion on the lake, while the sepoys were cooking their fish, and reiterated his whine about the devildom of the country into which the Englishman had dragged him. *Padre Martum Sahib* would never have thus treated the owner of sixteen horses, all fast and big ones, and eight superior "shutin tongas." "Let us get away," said Ram Baksh. "You are not here for *shikar,* and the water is very bad." It was indeed, except when taken from the lake, and then it only tasted fishy. "We will go, Ram Baksh," said the Englishman. "We will go in the very early morning, and in the meantime here is fish to stay your stomach with."

When a transparent *kanat,* which fails by

three feet to reach ceiling or floor, is the only bar between the East and the West, he would be a churl indeed who stood upon "invidious race distinctions." The Englishman went out and fraternised with the Military—the four-rupee soldiers of Boondi who guarded him. They were armed, one with an old Tower musket crazy as to nipple and hammer, one with a native-made smooth-bore, and one with a composite contrivance—English sporting muzzle-loader stock with a compartment for a jointed cleaning-rod, and hammered octagonal native barrel, wire-fastened, with a tuft of cotton on the foresight. All three guns were loaded, and the owners were very proud of them. They were simple folk, these men at arms, with an inordinate appetite for broiled fish. They were not *always* soldiers they explained. They cultivated their crops until wanted for any duty that might turn up. They were paid, now and again, at intervals, but they were paid in coin and not in kind.

The *munshis* and the vakils and the runners had departed after seeing that the Englishman was safe for the night, so the freedom of the little gathering on the bund was unrestrained. The *chowkidar* came out of his cave into the firelight. Warm wood ashes, by the way, like

Epp's cocoa, are "grateful and comforting" to cold toes. He took a fish and incontinently choked, for he was a feeble old man. Set right again, he launched into a very long and quite unintelligible story while the sepoys said reverently:—"He is an old man and remembers many things." As he babbled, the night shut in upon the lake and the valley of Boondi. The last cows were driven into the water for their evening drink, the waterfowl and the monkeys went to bed, and the stars came out and made a new firmament in the untroubled bosom of the lake. The light of the fire showed the ruled line of the bund springing out of the soft darkness of the wooded hill on the left and disappearing into the solid darkness of the bare hill on the right. Below the bund a man cried aloud to keep wandering pigs from the gardens whose tree-tops rose to a level with the bund-edge. Beyond the trees all was swaddled in gloom. When the gentle buzz of the unseen city died out, it seemed as though the bund were the very Swordwide Bridge that runs, as every one knows, between this world and the next. The water lapped and muttered, and now and again a fish jumped, with the shatter of broken glass, blurring the peace of the reflected heavens.

"And duller should I be than some fat weed
That rots itself at ease on Lethe's wharf."

The poet who wrote those lines knew nothing whatever of Lethe's wharf. The Englishman had found it, and it seemed to him, at that hour and in that place, that it would be good and desirable never to return to the Commissioners and the Deputy Commissioners any more, but to lie at ease on the warm sunlit bund by day, and, at night, near a shadow-breeding fire, to listen for the strangled voices and whispers of the darkness in the hills; thus after as long a life as the *chowkidar's,* dying easily and pleasantly, and being buried in a red tomb on the borders of the lake. Surely no one would come to reclaim him, across those weary, weary miles of rock-strewn road.... "And this," said the *chowkidar,* raising his voice to enforce attention, "is true talk. Everybody knows it, and now the Sahib knows it. I am an old man." He fell asleep at once, with his hand on the *chillam* that was doing duty for a whole *hukka* among the company. He had been talking for nearly a quarter of an hour.

See how great a man is the true novelist! Six or seven thousand miles away, Walter Besant of the Golden Pen had created Mr. Maliphant —the ancient of figureheads, in *All Sorts and*

Conditions of Men, and here, in Boondi, the Englishman had found Mr. Maliphant in the withered flesh. So he drank Walter Besant's health in the water of the Burra Talao. One of the sepoys turned himself round, with a clatter of accoutrements, shifted his blanket under his elbow, and told a tale. It had something to do with his *khet,* and a *gunna* which certainly was not sugar-cane. It was elusive. At times it seemed that it was a woman, then changed to a right of way, and lastly appeared to be a tax; but the more he attempted to get at its meaning through the curious patois in which its doings or its merits were enveloped, the more dazed the Englishman became. None the less the story was a fine one, embellished with much dramatic gesture which told powerfully against the fire-light. Then the second sepoy, who had been enjoying the *chillam* all the time, told a tale, the purport of which was that the dead in the tombs round the lake were wont to get up of nights and *shikar*. This was a fine and ghostly story; and its dismal effect was much heightened by some clamour of the night far up the lake beyond the floor of stars.

The third sepoy said nothing. He had eaten too much fish and was fast asleep by the side of the *chowkidar*.

They were all Mahomedans, and consequently all easy to deal with. A Hindu is an excellent person, but....but....there is no knowing what is in his heart, and he is hedged about with so many strange observances.

The Hindu or Mahomedan bent, which each Englishman's mind must take before he has been three years in the country is, of course, influenced by Province or Presidency. In Rajputana generally, the Political swears by the Hindu, and holds that the Mahomedan is untrustworthy. But a man who will eat with you and take your tobacco, sinking the fiction that it has been doctored with *shrab,* cannot be very bad after all.

That night when the tales were all told and the guard, bless them, were snoring peaceably in the starlight, a man came stealthily into the enclosure of *kanats* and woke the Englishman by muttering *Sahib, Sahib* in his ear. It was no robber but some poor devil with a petition—a grimy, welted paper. He was absolutely unintelligible, and additionally so in that he stammered almost to dumbness. He stood by the bed, alternately bowing to the earth and standing erect, his arms spread aloft, and his whole body working as he tried to force out some rebellious word in a key that should not wake the men without. What could the Englishman do? He was no Government servant, and had no concern with *urzis.* It was laughable to lie in a warm bed and watch this unfortunate heathen, clicking and choking and gasping in his desperate desire to make the *Sahib* understand. It was also unpleasantly pathetic, and the listener found himself as blindly striving to catch the meaning as the pleader to make himself comprehended. But it was no use; and in the end the man departed as he had come—bowed, abject, and unintelligible.

Let every word written against Ganesh be rescinded. It was by his ordering that the Englishman saw such a dawn on the Burra Talao as he had never before set eyes on. Every fair morning is a reprint, blurred perhaps, of the opening of the First Day; but this splendour was a thing to be put aside from all other days and remembered. The stars had no fire in them and the fish had stopped jumping, when the black water of the lake paled and grew grey. While he watched, it seemed to the Englishman that some voice on the hills were intoning the first verses of Genesis. The grey light moved on the face of the waters till, with no interval, a blood-red glare shot up from the horizon and, inky black against the intense red, a giant crane floated out towards the sun. In the still shadowed city the great Palace drum boomed and throbbed to show that the gates were open, while the dawn swept up the valley and made all things clear. The blind man who said:—"The blast of a trumpet is red" spoke only the truth. The breaking of the red dawn is like the blast of a trumpet.

"What," said the *chowkidar,* picking the ashes of the overnight fire out of his beard, "what, I say, are five eggs or twelve eggs to such a Raj as ours? What also are fowls—what are"—....."There was no talk of fowls. Where is the fowl-man from whom you got the eggs?" "He is here. No, he is there. I do not know. I am an old man, and I and the Raj supply everything without price. The *murghiwalla* will be paid by the State—liberally paid. Let the *Sahib* be happy! *Wah! Wah!*"

Experience of *beegar* in Himalayan villages had made the Englishman very tender in raising supplies that were given *gratis;* but the *murghiwalla* could not be found, and the value of his wares was, later, paid to Ganesh—Ganesh of Situr, for that is the name of the village full of priests, through which the Englishman had passed in ignorance two days before. A double handful of sweet smelling flowers made the receipt.

Boondi was wide awake before half-pastseven in the morning. Her hunters, on foot and on horse, were filing towards the Deoli Gate to go *shikarring.* They would hunt tiger and deer they said, even with matchlocks and muzzle-loaders as uncouth as those the *Sahib* saw. They were a merry company and chaffed the Quarter-Guard at the gate unmercifully when a bullock-cart, laden with the cases of the "Batoum Naphtha and Oil Company" blocked the road. One of them had been a soldier of the Queen, and, excited by the appearance of a *Sahib,* did so rebuke and badger the Quarter-Guard for their slovenliness that they threatened to come out of the barracks and destroy him.

So, after one last look at the Palace high up the hill side, the Englishman was borne away along the Deoli road. The peculiarity of Boondi is the peculiarity of the covered pitfall. One does not see it till one falls into it. A quarter of a mile from the gate, it and its Palace were invisible. The runners who had chivalrously volunteered to protect the wanderer against possible dacoits had been satisfactorily disposed of, and all was peace and unruffled loaferdom. But the Englishman was grieved at heart. He had fallen in love with Boondi the beautiful, and believed that he would never again see anything half so fair. The utter untouchedness of the town was one-half the charm and its associations the other. Read Tod, who is far too good to be chipped or sampled, read Tod luxuriously on the bund of the Burra Talao, and the spirit of the place will enter into you and you will be happy.

To enjoy life thoroughly, haste and bustle must be abandoned. Ram Baksh has said that Englishmen are always *dikking* to go forward, and for this reason, though beyond doubt they pay well and readily, are not wise men. He gave utterance to this philosophy after he had mistaken his road and pulled up in what must have been a disused quarry hard by a cane-field. There were patches and pockets of cultivation along the rocky road, where men grew cotton, *til,* chillies, tobacco, and sugar-cane. "I will get you sugar-cane," said Ram Baksh. "Then we will go forward, and perhaps some of these jungly fools will tell us where the road is." A "jungly fool," a tender of goats, did in time appear, but there was no hurry; the sugar-cane was sweet and purple and the sun warm.

The Englishman lay out at high noon on the crest of a rolling upland crowned with rock, and heard, as a loafer had told him he would hear, the "set of the day," which is as easily discernible as the change of tone between the rising and the falling tide. At a certain hour the impetus of the morning dies out, and all things, living and inanimate, turn their thoughts to the prophecy of the coming night. The little wandering breezes drop for a time, and, when they blow afresh, bring the message. The "set of the day" as the loafer said, has changed, the machinery is beginning to run down, the unseen tides of the air are falling. The moment of the change can only be felt in the open and in touch with the earth, and once discovered, seem to place the finder in deep accord and fellowship with all things on the earth. Perhaps this is why the genuine loafer, though "frequently drunk," is "always polite to the stranger," and shows such a genial tolerance towards the weaknesses of mankind, black, white, or brown.

In the evening when the jackals were scuttling across the roads and the cranes had gone to roost, came Deoli the desolate, and an unpleasant meeting. Six days away from his kind had bred in a Cockney heart a great desire to see an Englishman again. An elaborate loaf through the cantonment—fifteen minutes' walk from end to end—showed only one distant dog-cart and a small English child with an ayah. There was grass in the soldierly-straight roads, and some of the cross-cuts had never been used at all from the days when the cantonment had been first laid out. In the western corner lay the cemetery—the only carefully-tended and newly-whitewashed thing in this God-forgotten place. Some years ago a man had said good-bye to the Englishman; adding cheerily:—"We shall meet again. The world's a very little place y'know." His prophecy was a true one, for the two met indeed, but the prophet was lying in Deoli Cemetery near the well, which is decorated so ecclesiastically with funeral urns. Truly the world is a *very* little place that a man should so stumble upon dead acquaintances when he goes abroad.

THE LAST.

Comes back to the Railway, after Reflections on the Management of the Empire; and so Home again, with apology to all who have read thus far.

IN the morning the tonga rattled past Deoli Cemetery into the open, where the Deoli Irregulars were drilling. They marked the beginning of civilisation and white shirts; for which reason they seemed altogether detestable. Yet another day's jolting, enlivened by the philosophy of Ram Baksh, and then came Nasirabad. The last pair of ponies suggested serious thought. They had covered eighteen miles at an average speed of eight miles an hour, and were well conditioned little rats. "A Colonel Sahib gave me this one for *bakshish*," said Ram Baksh, flicking the near one. "It was his *baba's* pony. The *baba* was five years old. When he went away, the Colonel Sahib said:—'Ram Baksh, you are a good man. Never have I seen such a good man. This horse is yours.'" Ram Baksh was getting a horse's work out of a child's pony. Surely we in India work the land much as the Colonel Sahib worked his son's mount; making it do child's work when so much more can be screwed out of it. A native and a native State deals otherwise with horse and holding. Perhaps our extreme scrupulousness in handling may be Statecraft, but, after even a short sojourn in places which are dealt with not so tenderly, it seems absurd. There are States where things are done, and done without protest, that would make the hair of the educated native stand on end with horror. These things are of course not expedient to write; because their publication would give a great deal of unnecessary pain and heart-searching to estimable native administrators who have the hope of a Star before their eyes, and would not better matters in the least.

Note this fact though. With the exception of such journals as, occupying a central position in British territory, levy blackmail from the neighbouring States, there are no independent papers in Rajputana. A King may start a weekly, to encourage a taste for Sanskrit and high Hindi, or a Prince may create a Court Chronicle; but that is all. A "free press" is not allowed, and this the native journalist knows. With good management he can, keeping under the shadow of our flag, raise two hundred rupees from a big man here, and five hundred from a rich man there, but he does not establish himself across the Border. To one who has reason to hold a stubborn disbelief in even the elementary morality of the native press, this bashfulness and lack of enterprise is amusing. But to return to the over-the-way administrations. There is nothing exactly wrong in the methods of government that are overlaid with English terms and forms. They are vigorous, in certain points, and where they are not vigorous, there is a cheery happy-go-luckiness about the arrangement that must be seen to be understood. The shift and play of a man's fortune across the Border is as sudden as anything in the days of Haroun-al-Raschid of blessed memory, and there are stories, to be got for the unearthing, as wild and as improbable as those in the *Thousand and One Nights*. Most impressive of all is the way in which the country is "used," and its elasticity under pressure. In the good old days the Durbar raised everything it could from the people, and the King spent as much as ever he could on his personal pleasures. Now the institution of the Political has stopped the grabbing, for which, by the way, some of the monarchs are not in the least grateful—and smoothed the outward face of things. But there is still a difference, and such a difference, between our ways and the ways of the other places. A year spent among native States ought to send a man back to the Decencies and the Law Courts and the Rights of the Subject with a supreme contempt for those who rave about the oppressions of the brutal bureaucrat. One month nearly taught an average Englishman that it was the proper thing to smite anybody of mean aspect and obstructive tendencies on the mouth with a shoe. Hear what an intelligent loafer said. His words are at least as valuable as these babblings. He was, as usual, wonderfully drunk, and the gift of speech came down upon him. The conversation—he was a great politician this loafer—had turned on the poverty of India:—"Poor!" said he. "Of course it's poor. Oh yes! D—d poor! And I'm poor, an' you're poor, altogether. Do you expect people will give you money without you ask 'em? No. I tell you, Sir, there's enough money in India to pave *Hell* with if you could only get at it. I've kep' servants in my day. Did they ever leave me without a hundred or a hundred and fifty put by—and never touched? *You mark that.* Does any black man who has been in Guv'ment service go away without hundreds an' hundreds put by—and never touched? You mark that. Money! The place stinks o' money—just kept out o' sight. Do you ever know a native that didn't say *Garib admi?* They've been sayin' *Garib admi* so long that the Guv'ment learns to believe 'em, and now they're all bein' treated as though they was paupers. I'm a pauper, an' you're a pauper—we 'aven't got anything hid in the ground—an' so's every white man in this forsaken country. But the Injian he's a rich man. How do I know? Because I've tramped on foot, or warrant pretty well from one end of the place to the other, an' I know what I'm talkin' about, and this ere Guv'ment goes peckin' an' fiddlin' over its tuppenny-ha'penny little taxes as if it was afraid. Which it is. You see how they do things in ——. It's six sowars here, and ten sowars there, and—'Pay up, you brutes, or we'll pull your ears over your head.' And when they've taken all they can get, the headman, he says:—'This is a dashed poor yield. I'll come again.' *Of course* the people digs up something out of the ground, and they pay. I know the way it's done, and that's the way to do it. You can't go to an Injian an' say:—'Look here. Can you pay me five rupees?' He says:—'*Garib admi,*' of course, an' would say it if he was as rich as a banker. But if you send half a dozen sowars at him and shift the thatch off of his roof, he'll pay. Guv'ment can't do that. I don't suppose it could. There is no reason why it shouldn't. But it might do something like it, to show that it wasn't going to have no nonsense. Why, I'd undertake to raise a hundred million —what am I talking of?—a hundred and fifty million pounds from this country *per annum*, and it wouldn't be strained *then*. One hundred and fifty millions you could raise as easy as paint, if you just made these ere Injians understand that they had to pay an' make no bones about it. It's enough to make a man sick to go in over yonder to —— and see what they do; and then come back an' see what we do. Perfectly sickenin' it is. Borrer money! Why the country could pay herself an' everything she wants, if she was only made to do it. It's this bloomin' *Garib admi* swindle that's been going on all these years, that has made fools o' the Guv'ment." Then he became egoistical, this ragged ruffian who conceived that he knew the road to illimitable wealth, and told the story of his life, interspersed with anecdotes that would blister the paper they were written on. But through all his ravings, he stuck to his hundred-and-fifty-million-theory, and though the listener dissented from him and the brutal cruelty with which his views were stated, an unscientific impression remained and was not to be shaken off. Across the Border one feels that the country is being used, exploited, "made to sit up," so to speak. In our territories the feeling is equally strong of wealth "just round the corner," as the loafer said, and a people wrapped up in cotton wool and ungetatable. Will any man, who really knows something of a little piece of India and has not the fear of running counter to custom before his eyes, explain how this impression is produced, and why it is an erroneous one? This digression has taken us far from the child's pony of Ram Baksh.

Nasirabad marked the end of the Englishman's holiday, and there was sorrow in his heart. "Come back again," said Ram Baksh cheerfully, "and bring a gun with you. Then I'll take you to Gungra, and I'll drive you myself. Drive you just as well as I've driven these four days past." An amicable open-minded soul was Ram Baksh. May his tongas never grow less.

"This 'ere Burma fever is a bad thing to have. It's pulled me down awful; an' now I am going to Peshawar. *Are* you the Station-Master?" It was Thomas—white cheeked, sunken-eyed, drawn-mouthed Thomas—travelling from Nasirabad to Peshawar on pass; and with him was a Corporal new to his stripes and doing station duty. Every Thomas is interesting, except when he is too drunk to speak. This Thomas was an enthusiast. He had volunteered, from a Home-going regiment shattered by Burma fever, into a regiment at Peshawar, had broken down at Nasirabad on his way up with his draft, and was now journeying into the unknown to pick up another medal. "There's sure to be something on the Frontier," said this gaunt, haggard boy—he was little more, though he reckoned four years' service and considered himself somebody. "When there's anything going, Peshawar's the place to be in, they tell me; but I hear we shall have to march down to Calcutta in no time." The Corporal was a little man and showed his friend off with great pride:—"Ah, you should have come to us," said he; "we're the regiment, we are." "Well, I went with the rest of our men," said Thomas. "There's three hundred of us volunteered to stay on, and we all went for the same regiment. Not but what I'm saying yours is a good regiment," he added with grave courtesy. This loosed the Corporal's tongue, and he discanted on the virtues of the regiment and the merits of the officers. It has been written that Thomas is devoid of *esprit de corps,* because of the jerkiness of the arrangements under which he now serves. If this be true, he manages to conceal his feelings very well; for he speaks most fluently in praise of his own regiment; and, for all his youth, has a keen appreciation of the merits of his officers. Go to him when his heart is opened, and hear him going through the roll of the subalterns, by a grading totally unknown in the *Army List,* and you will pick up something worth the hearing. Thomas, with the Burma fever on him, tried to cut in, from time to time, with stories of his officers and what they had done "when we was marchin' all up and down Burma," but the little Corporal went on gaily.

They made a curious contrast—these two types. The lathy, town-bred Thomas with hock-bottle shoulders, a little education, and a keen desire to get more medals and stripes; and the little, deep-chested, bull-necked Corporal brimming over with vitality and devoid of any ideas beyond the "regiment." And the end of both lives, in all likelihood, would be a nameless grave in some cantonment burying-ground, with, if the case were specially interesting and the Regimental Doctor had a turn for the pen, an obituary notice in the *Indian Medical Journal.* It was an unpleasant thought.

From the Army to the Navy is a perfectly natural transition, but one hardly to be expected in the heart of India. Dawn showed the railway carriage full of riotous boys, for the Agra and Mount Abu schools had broken up for holidays. Surely it was natural enough to ask a child—not a boy, but a child—whether he was going home for the holidays; and surely it was a crushing, a petrifying thing, to hear in a clear treble, tinged with icy *hauteur*:—"No! I'm on leave. I'm a midshipman." Two "officers of Her Majesty's Navy"—mids of a man-o'-war in Bombay —— were going Up-country on ten days' leave! They had not travelled much more than twice round the world; but they should have printed the fact on a label. They chattered like daws, and their talk was as a whiff of fresh air from the open sea, while the train ran eastward under the Aravalis. At that hour their lives were bound up in and made glorious by the hope of riding a horse when they reached their journey's end. Much had they seen "cities and men," and the artless way in which they interlarded their conversation with allusions to "one of these shore-going chaps you see" was delicious. They had no cares, no fears, no servants, and an unlimited stock of wonder and admiration for everything they saw, from the "cute little well-scoops" to a herd of deer grazing on the horizon. It was not until they had opened their young hearts with infantine abandon that the listener could guess from the incidental *argot* where these pocket-Ulysseses had travelled. South African, Norwegian, and Arabian words were used to help out the slang of Haslar, and a copious vocabulary of shipboard terms, complicated with modern Greek. As free from self-consciousness as children, as ignorant as beings from another planet of the Anglo-Indian life into which they were going to dip for a few days, shrewd and observant as befits men of the world who have authority, and neat-handed and resourceful as—blue-jackets, they were a delightful study, and accepted freely and frankly the elaborate apologies tendered to them for the unfortunate mistake about the "holidays." The roads divided and they went their way; and there was a shadow after they had gone, for the Globe-Trotter said to his wife:—"What I like about Jeypore"—accent on the first syllable, if you please—"is its characteristic easternness." And the Globe-Trotter's wife said, "Yes! It is purely Oriental."

This was Jeypore with the gas-jets and the water-pipes as was shown at the beginning of these trivial letters; and the Globe-Trotter and his wife had not been to Amber. Joyful thought! They had not seen the soft splendour of Udaipur, the night-mare of Chitor, the grim power of Jodhpur and the virgin beauty of Boondi—fairest of all places that the Englishman had set eyes on. The Globe-Trotter was great in the matter of hotels and food, but he had not lain under the shadow of a tonga in soft warm sand, eating cold pork with a pocket-knife and thanking Providence who put sweet-water streams where wayfarers wanted them. He had not drunk out the brilliant cold-weather night in the company of a King of loafers, a grimy scallawag with a six days' beard and an unholy knowledge of native States. He had attended service in cantonment churches; but he had not known what it was to witness the simple solemn ceremonial in the dining-room of a far away Residency, when all the English folk within a hundred-mile circuit bowed their heads before the God of the Christians. He had blundered about temples of strange deities with a guide at his elbow; but he had not known what it was to attempt conversation with a temple dancing-girl (*not* such an one as Edwin Arnold invented), and to be rewarded for a misturned compliment with a deftly heaved bunch of marigold buds on his respectable bosom. Yes, he had undoubtedly lost much, and the measure of his loss was proven in his estimate of the Orientalism of Jeypore.

But what had he who sat in judgment upon him gained? One perfect month of loaferdom, to be remembered above all others, and the night of the visit to Chitor, to be remembered even when the month is forgotten. Also the sad knowledge that of all the fair things seen, the inept pen gives but a feeble and blurred picture.

Let those who have read to the end, pardon a hundred blemishes.